GOALKEEPING

Alex Welsh

A & C Black · London

*In memory of my mother
who lovingly washed countless
filthy football kits.*

First published 1990 by
A & C Black (Publishers) Limited
35 Bedford Row, London WC1R 4JH

© 1990 Alex Welsh

ISBN 0 7136 5789 8

A CIP catalogue record for this book is available from
the British Library.

Typeset by August Filmsetting, Haydock, St Helens

Illustration acknowledgements
Photographs by Mike Chittleborough; line drawings by
Taurus Graphics.

Printed and bound in Great Britain by
BPCC Hazell Books, Aylesbury, Bucks

Contents

Foreword

I am very pleased that a book has been written on goalkeeping. The goal-keeper's position is a specialist one and has rightly been the subject of great discussion in the last few years. During my football lifetime, the status of the goalkeeper has risen from that of 'just another player' to one of great importance to the overall success or failure of the team. This is borne out by the escalating transfer fees being paid by football clubs for quality goalkeepers. Our top keepers have emerged as role models for a vast number of up and coming footballers who from an early age have sought glory from playing between the sticks.

For too many years the need to improve the quality of goalkeeping coaching has been neglected and it is encouraging to read a book which seeks to fill this gap in our footballing knowledge. The problem has been that the goalkeeper has been used as a stopper of shots for forwards' practices rather than as someone who requires individual attention. As the author emphasises, goalkeeping coaching should revolve around improving technique and decision making.

From a manager's standpoint, I feel that although the keeper is a specialist, he cannot afford to be an individual with regard to the team's pattern of play. His privileged view of the whole pitch means that he is a vital member of the defensive unit in terms of playing as an extra sweeper and also as a source of important information.

Goalkeeping will be very useful for professional and amateur coaches and players alike as I believe that at every level most of us would confess to not being aware of all the possibilities and variations of goalkeeper training.

Having read Alex Welsh's book, I am totally convinced of the worth of specialist goalkeeping training. A team that ignores the coaching of its goal-keeper does so at its own peril.

Stephen Perryman

Acknowledgements

I would like to thank Teresa Wiseman (*Friends of Fulham FC and England*), Perry Suckling (*Crystal Palace FC and England U21's*) and Mick Payne (*Tottenham Hotspur FC*) for their invaluable contributions to this book.

I am also greatly indebted to Bob Wilson and Mick Payne who have been a tremendous source of knowledge, ideas and inspiration.

However, it is to my wife, Maria, that I am most grateful. I would like to thank her for her help and encouragement in this venture and, above all, for her unfailing understanding of my obsession with football.

Introduction

I would like to dispel the myth that 'goalkeepers are mad'. They are just a breed apart. Keeping goal is a highly technical and recently much valued job. The number of specialised coaches on the professional circuit and the increase in transfer fees demanded for goalkeepers supports this view. The 'mad' label reflects the individualised nature of the job and the lengths to which the keeper will go to protect his goal. Most of the goalkeepers I have met place a clean sheet before personal safety, and therefore those people who do not share the obsession are driven to question their sanity.

This commonality of purpose has led to the development of genuine camaraderie between goalkeepers. It is often said that they are the keenest of rivals but the best of friends, and this is true. After a match goalkeepers often get together to chat about aspects of their craft in a way that outfield players do not.

Another saying that sums up the lot of the goalkeeper is that football is a team game until he makes a mistake; then it becomes an individual sport. There is little doubt that the position of goalkeeper is the most pressurised on the field and often the loneliest. All players will make errors, but the keeper's usually result in a goal conceded. Once he manages to keep his mistakes to a minimum and proves his reliability his work will be measured by the important saves he makes. Good goalkeepers put their mistakes behind them and learn from the experience. One mistake does not make a bad goalkeeper, or one save a good goalkeeper. So, what are the factors that make the good goalkeeper stand out from the crowd?

Note
Throughout the text coaches and players are, in the main referred to as 'he'. This should, of course, be taken to mean 'he or she' where appropriate.

Qualities of the goalkeeper

Natural ability

Natural ability is important, but it needs to be combined with hard work, good coaching and appropriate match experience. It is very difficult to define natural ability or talent, but when I see a young goalkeeper for the first time I look carefully at his handling skills. The equivalent to this for an outfield player would be his control or 'touch'. Handling is the fundamental skill of goal-keeping and without the basic ability to judge the flight of a ball and execute a successful catch, little progress will be made.

Competitiveness

The next aspect that I look for is competitiveness; how much does the keeper want to prevent the ball going into the net? The extent to which the player does not want to be beaten will determine how hard he will work to improve his craft. If the young keeper is going to make it to the top he should strive relentlessly to polish his strengths and minimise his weaknesses. This, of course, will involve some degree of self-assessment and it is imperative that the keeper is totally honest with himself.

The role of the coach

The perceptive coach will be able to observe his goalkeeper's match perform-ance and isolate areas that require special attention during training. Coaching tailored to the individual needs of the keeper will help him grow in confidence and competence.

Gaining match experience

Appropriate match experience is essential if the goalkeeper is to develop in the right way. Ideally the player should not be performing at a standard where he is too comfortable. If his potential is to be fulfilled, the demands placed on him should be challenging. This may involve playing promising youngsters above their age group. The coach must remember that actual match practice is the richest learning environment.

This book will examine thoroughly the goalkeeper's craft and provide practices that will allow concentrated rehearsal of a particular skill or technique. Starting at the most basic level and increasing in difficulty, these practices are accompanied by appropriate coaching points which will help to facilitate the learning process. The key to success is the application of sound basic techniques and good decision making, and these factors should be reinforced constantly.

1 Coaching goalkeepers

Coaches at all levels need to be well equipped to look after their goalkeepers. It has been said that it takes a goalkeeper to coach a goalkeeper and there is some truth in this. Aside from the technical input of the coach, he must understand what it is like to play in that position. Ironically, however, you can be the greatest goalkeeper in the world and yet be ineffective as a coach. This is because the whole purpose of coaching is to bring out the best in other players.

What makes an effective coach?

The prerequisites of coaching are a sound knowledge of the subject and an understanding of the players involved. Hopefully the first requirement will be met after reading this book! The consequences of imparting incorrect information could be disastrous, so it is important that the coach is conversant with the subject matter. If the coach is to apply his knowledge and experience successfully he must know his keeper's capabilities and have an awareness of how players learn. Coaching is not an opportunity for the coach to show how clever he is. It is a means to an end, the end being improved match performance. Therefore, the actual coaching process should reflect the needs of the player. Equipped with this knowledge of both player and subject, the coach should devise a coaching schedule aimed at improving match play.

The coaching programme

There are obvious factors such as age and level of ability which will determine how sophisticated the coaching programme will be. However, as a general rule all goalkeepers should work at reducing the number of mistakes in their game. As mistakes are attributable to either a momentary lapse in basic technique or an incorrect decision, each training session should incorporate practices aimed at ingraining good handling and footwork skills. Also, where possible the coach should arrange for simulated match practice where the keeper has to choose whether to leave or to stay on his goal-line. Constant work on the basics will increase the goalkeeper's reliability and hence his value to the team.

As far as minimising weaknesses is concerned, the coach should be able to diagnose key faults in players' performances and then set up a coaching situation which allows for concentrated practice on a particular aspect. To do this he must be aware of the sequential nature of coaching and start at a level where the keeper can achieve success.

Coaching points

Throughout the session the main coaching points should be clear, concise and relevant so that the keeper can easily digest them. Where appropriate these key factors should be accompanied by a demonstration, because a visual explanation can speak a thousand words. The goalkeeper then practises the correct technique until it is performed successfully. As competence and confidence grow, the practice increases in difficulty and realism.

For example, if a goalkeeper is having difficulty in dealing with high crosses during games, it would be inadvisable to begin the practice with the penalty area full of players. It would benefit both the player and the coach to commence with an unopposed practice where the keeper could be observed fielding crosses in isolation. Once satisfied that the basic technique is sound and that the keeper is achieving success the coach can, by introducing defenders and then attackers, assess his player's decision making and technique under more realistic circumstances.

At each stage of the progression it is essential that the keeper is regularly experiencing success before moving on to a more difficult situation. Hopefully by the end of the session the goalkeeper will be performing effectively under simulated match conditions.

A cautionary note

Goalkeeping coaching is not solely about exercises designed to have the keeper diving at great speed all over the place. There is a place for pressure training as part of the conditioning and fitness process, but there are very few occasions during actual matches when the keeper is faced with a barrage of shots. More importantly, the coach must remember that technique breaks down when fatigue sets in. If the practice is intended to improve technique, then the keeper should be allowed to recover between each save. Forcing the player to react in an unrealistic way might result in a rushed technique and ultimately in the development of bad habits.

Confidence-building

In addition to the technical aspects of coaching, one area which merits considerable attention is confidence. As the last line of defence, the keeper has to have total faith in his ability. Success breeds confidence and there is no better feeling than being right on form. However, it is when things are not going well that the mental toughness of the goalkeeper is tested. The attitude of the coach in this situation can make or break the keeper. The wise coach will sense his player's unease and will spend time with him, analysing those aspects of his game that cause most concern. Above all, the coach must make the player feel valued despite his loss of form.

Through progressive practices in training and an outward display of trust in his keeper's ability it will not be long before full confidence and form are restored. Often a public stand by the coach can allay the fears of team-mates who begin to doubt the ability of their keeper. Players will respond better to a coach who respects their talents.

To summarise, the coaching process involves the following stages:
(a) knowledge of subject matter
(b) understanding the goalkeeper
(c) diagnosing key faults
(d) organising progressive practices related to the keeper's needs
(e) inspiring the goalkeeper with confidence
(f) improving match performance.

2 Match preparation

One of the great mysteries of football (and indeed one of its attractions) is that nothing is certain. There is always the chance that the unexpected may happen. This reflects the fact that all teams and their players are fallible and cannot maintain excellent form for every game. If a coach could market the unknown factor that is responsible for a great performance one week and a mediocre one the next, he would make a fortune. If the training is basically the same, week in week out, what is it that accounts for this inconsistency? The obvious answers are luck or the quality of opposition but the coach is powerless to affect both these factors.

However, one of the aspects related to consistency that the coach or player can influence is match preparation. Match preparation entails approaching the game with the right mental attitude and in an optimum state of physical readiness. Having reached this desired level of preparedness, it is essential that this condition is maintained throughout the match. The keeper should not lose concentration or allow himself to get cold. He should stay 'switched on' at all times.

Mental preparation

Mental rehearsal before matches is as important as the physical warm-up. The goalkeeper should visualise previous situations in which he has played well and relive them in his mind. By doing this he will approach the game in a positive manner. This type of mental preparation is useful in restoring confidence after a mistake in a previous game. All negative thoughts should be banished as the goalkeeper imagines himself making a string of tremendous saves.

Once into the game no keeper will be too upset by the shot that flies into the top right-hand corner, but he will lose sleep over the back pass that trickles through his legs. The goalkeeper must aim to eradicate the costly mistakes from his game. If a goal is to be conceded, it should be due to brilliance on the part of the opponents, a defensive blunder in front of him or a fluke. When this aim is realised on a regular basis the reliability of the keeper will be confirmed and confidence will spread throughout the team.

How does the keeper avoid letting in the 'soft' goal? Much depends upon combining good basic technique with the right attitude. The way in which the keeper approaches a game should not alter because of the quality of the opposition. Time and time again throughout the history of football supposedly superior sides have come unstuck because they underestimated the other team. Thus the goalkeeper should remember the old adage 'Treat every shot with respect'. By religiously following this motto, concentration on the basics will be enhanced and, in turn, the number of errors will be greatly reduced.

However, despite this resolution the odd mistake will still be made. The way in which the keeper responds after making a mistake is crucial. None of us can change history, so it is important to put mistakes at the back of your mind and get on with the rest of the match. Dwelling on mistakes during the game will affect confidence and concentration. Mistakes can be analysed afterwards and used as a learning experience. After all, we are only human and therefore prone to the odd lapse. In short, aim for perfection but do not expect it all of the time.

There are three basic types of reaction to making a mistake.

(a) Confidence crumbles. Due to one mistake the keeper loses all faith in his ability, and the positive attitude with which he began the match evaporates rapidly. Further situations similar to the one in which the error occurred fill him with terror. His obvious state of nervousness is recognised both by the opposition, who exploit it, and by his own team who lose confidence in him.

(b) The goalkeeper tries too hard. In an attempt to atone for his error the keeper attempts to involve himself in situations against his better judgement. Rather than allowing play to develop and dealing with problems in the appropriate manner he makes rash decisions in order to get to the ball quickly. He feels the need to redeem himself immediately.

(c) The keeper permits himself only a moment's self-indulgence and gets on with the remainder of the game, determined not to allow the error to affect his confidence or concentration.

For the goalkeeper who responds as in (a) and (b) one mistake can lead to another and, eventually, to a loss of form. The goalkeeper who can handle set-backs is the one who knows that one mistake does not make a bad player.

Physical preparation

Physical preparation for matches or training has three objectives:

(a) to put all muscle groups likely to be used in match play through full stretch
(b) to exercise sufficiently the heart so that blood is delivered rapidly around the system, thereby raising the base body temperature
(c) to give the keeper handling experience of the type he is likely to face in the game.

The warm-up should start slowly and gently with stretches, move on to more vigorous running and jumping exercises and then conclude with handling practice. Most footballers are creatures of habit (bordering on the superstitious) and usually follow the same routine before a match. If their warm-up satisfies the aforementioned objectives and results in consistently good performances, then nothing should be changed.

Exercises

The exercises and practices listed below are by no means comprehensive but may be useful as a general guide.

Static stretching
Warning: at the beginning of a warm-up all stretches should be done slowly and players should not 'bounce' into exercises.

(i) On tiptoes with arms stretched above the head. Come down slowly, pushing arms backwards and returning them to the side. Five repetitions.
(ii) Lying face-down, place the forearms in front of the body and gently arch the back. Return to the supine position. Five repetitions.
(iii) Standing with the legs apart, hold the arms in the twelve o'clock position and then slowly move the hands around the clock (bending at the hips where necessary). Three repetitions in each direction.
(iv) Try to force the heel of the back foot flat on the ground whilst leaning the upper body forwards. Three repetitions on each leg. (See calf stretch illustration opposite.)
(v) With the legs together, bend at the knees and clasp the toes. Slowly straighten the legs with the fingers still holding the toes. Five repetitions.
(vi) Hold the right foot with the right hand and bend at the knee so that the heel reaches up to the lower back. Five repetitions on each leg.

Groin stretch.

Calf stretch.

(vii)   With legs apart and feet pointing forwards, shift the body-weight to one side so that a stretch is felt in the groin. Five repetitions.

(viii) Stand as if starting a race. Let the body sink downwards so that tension is felt along the thigh of the back leg. Five repetitions.

(ix)   With feet apart, lean down to one side. The nearest hand should reach towards the ankle, with the opposite hand over the head. Five repetitions for each side.

(x)   With legs apart and pelvis pushed forwards, arch the back to touch the left heel with the left hand. Repeat using right hand to right heel, then two hands simultaneously and finally opposite hand to opposite heel. Three repetitions of the whole process.

Ballistic exercises

(i)   Rotate the arms vigorously as in the butterfly swimming stroke for twenty seconds. Repeat the exercise using a backwards butterfly stroke.

(ii)   With legs fairly wide apart, touch the right ankle with the left hand and then the left ankle with the right hand. Carry on vigorously for twenty repetitions.

(iii)   Light jogging forwards, backwards and sideways.

(iv)   Light jogging
     (a)   bringing up the knees to the waist
     (b)   flicking the heels up to the buttocks
     (c)   flicking the heels up to touch the inside of the opposite thigh.

(v)   Three-quarter pace running 3 × 30 yds (3 × 27 m).

(vi)   Ten hops on each leg, looking for maximum distance each time.

(vii)   Ten bunny hops, looking for maximum height.

(viii) Five short sprints incorporating changes in direction.

(ix)   Five forward rolls.

(x)   Twenty press-ups.

Handling exercises

(i)   Roll the ball 3–4 yds (2.75–3.5 m) in front of you and sprint to pick it up whilst on the move. Five repetitions.

(ii)   Comfortable shots from 10–12 yds (9–11 m) to warm up the hands.

(iii)   Fielding crosses from both sides. (Throw the ball if the service is unreliable.)

(iv)   Concentrated handling. The server throws or volleys the ball from a distance of 8 yds (7.25 m). Twenty repetitions.

(v)   From a distance of 6–8 yds (5.5–7.25 m) the server passes the ball to the keeper's feet who has to react smartly to pick it up. Ten repetitions.

(vi)   From a distance of 6–8 yds (5.5–7.25 m) the server passes the ball to the side of the goalkeeper who has to glide across and pick it up. Ten repetitions.

(vii)   The keeper stands on the six-yard line and the server on the penalty spot. The server throws the ball over the head of the keeper who has to backpedal in order to make a catch. Five repetitions.

(viii) In a 4-yd (3.5 m) goal the server pushes the ball from a distance of 6–8 yds (5.5–7.25 m) to the side of the goalkeeper who dives to save. Five repetitions on each side.

(ix)   The server takes a variety of shots from the edge of the penalty area.

Whether the keeper chooses to use the above exercises or not, it is very important that he acclimatises himself with the ground and weather conditions. Handling practice in the goal-mouth will give him some indication of what type of bounce to expect and what influence the sun and wind might have.

The care of equipment

As befits his specialist position, the goalkeeper should possess a range of exclusive accessories. As part of his general preparation it is very important that he keeps his equipment in excellent working order.

Boots

As one slip can result in a goal conceded, the keeper should regularly check the length of his studs to ensure that they are appropriate for the prevailing ground conditions. This basically means short studs for hard surfaces and long ones for muddy surfaces.

Jersey and shorts

It is essential that these two items allow for the full range of movement. A loose-fitting jersey is preferable to one that is just the right size. Shoulder and elbow padding are a matter of personal choice since it is vital that the keeper feels comfortable. Such padding can be useful when ground conditions are hard. The wearing of an undershirt is advisable on cold days.

Track suit trousers

Track suit trousers (especially of the padded variety) are recommended for the icy grounds and bare goal-mouths played on towards the end of the season. The bane of goalkeepers' lives is the frequent friction burns inflicted on the outside of the upper thigh by diving on hard surfaces. Such injuries could be reduced by the wearing of protective track suit trousers. Once again, comfort and a full range of movement should determine which type is worn. If the keeper prefers not to wear trousers, then petroleum jelly smeared on the knees and thighs might reduce abrasions.

Cap

All goalkeepers should have a cap because it is a difficult skill catching in one hand whilst shielding the eyes from the sun with the other! The keeper should make sure the peak is large enough and that the cap does not fall off the head too easily.

Gloves

Warning: although goalkeeping gloves can considerably increase the effectiveness of handling, the keeper must not forget that it is the hands inside them that are important. Even though most gloves give an excellent grip, fingers and thumbs should still be spread well to the side and behind the ball (forming a 'W' shape) if the catch is to be 100 per cent safe.

Gloves will last longer and provide a better grip if they are well maintained. There are three steps to glove care.

(1)   Always wash gloves after matches in water not exceeding 86° F (30° C). A sponge will clean off surface dirt without causing abrasions to the latex palm. Do not use detergents.

(2)   After rinsing carefully with clean water allow the gloves to drip-dry away from direct heat or sunlight.

(3)   Dampening the latex palm before games will improve handling. When playing in muddy conditions it is recommended that the keeper takes a rag or a sponge out on to the field with him so that dirt can be removed from the palm when necessary.

3 Getting the basics right – head, hands, feet

When a keeper makes a mistake it is often attributable to a lapse in basic technique, such as taking the eye off the ball, poor handling or not moving the feet. Mastery of the basics will result in the goalkeeper making the difficult look easy and, more importantly, in helping to reduce the number of mistakes.

There is nothing more galling than to hear coaches or players console a keeper who has just made a glaring error by saying 'Unlucky!'. 'Unlucky' should refer to a deflection or some other kind of fluke and not to a lack of application of the basics. There are three basic or 'bread and butter' areas that require constant attention.

Hands

The keeper must be supremely confident in his hands. Strength work on forearms, wrists and fingers will assist this (*see* Chapter 12).

The keeper's hands should be in the ready position so that they can move quickly to deal with a sharp shot. The keeper should be prepared to lead with both hands (as if shackled by handcuffs) whenever possible. This entails ensuring that the hands are the first point of contact with the ball. Moving two hands in towards the flight of the ball will increase the probability of a safe catch. Also, the forearms may be used as shock absorbers to take the pace off the ball. By taking the ball in front of the eye line in this manner, the keeper allows himself some margin of error. Safe handling will be guaranteed if the fingers are well spread to the side and behind the ball so that a 'W' shape is formed by the hands.

Feet

Good footwork can make a difficult save look easy. Diving often involves a risk because for some time there is no barrier behind the hands. Moving quickly into line with the ball so that some part of the body is behind the hands will ensure that there is 'double cover'.

Safe handling means adopting the 'W' position, with the fingers and thumbs spread to the side and behind the ball.

When preparing to receive a shot the legs should be shoulder width apart, the knees slightly bent and the weight on the balls of the feet. If the legs are too wide apart it is difficult to achieve good spring and, of course, the ball might pass through them. When scooping up a ground shot the legs should move to less than a ball width apart. Whenever possible body-weight should be tipping forwards so that if the ball is mishandled a secondary save can be made almost immediately. If the ball is half saved and the keeper falls backwards, it takes longer to recover.

Speedy footwork is essential when diving for the ball. For those long-distance shots arrowing for the corners one or two quick steps before the dive will increase reach considerably. In contrast, fast shots close to the keeper necessitate the rapid collapsing of the legs if the ball is to be saved.

Head

The head should be rock steady so that the eyes are on the ball all of the time. At no point should the keeper turn his head away when making a save. Furthermore, it is very important to take the ball in front of the eye line so that it can always be seen.

Advice on serving

Before embarking on the coaching programme the coach should remember that, as the progressive practices are designed to allow the keeper concentrated rehearsal of a particular skill, sensible service is essential. Poor feeding starves the player of the right type of practice.

Handling

At all times the keeper should react to shots in training as he would in a match. If he drops the ball he should go for the secondary save immediately. Sloppiness in training will lead to sloppiness during matches.

Practice 1 (body shots)

The ball is thrown or volleyed towards the keeper's body from a distance of 6–10 yds (5.5–9 m).

Key points
(a) Adopt the ready position, that is, feet shoulder width apart, knees slightly bent, weight on balls of feet, hands ready (as if with handcuffs on).
(b) Cup ball into body.
(c) Stand firm – do not step backwards. See photograph overleaf.

The ready position. The goalkeeper is on the balls of his feet, his legs are shoulder width apart, his knees are slightly bent, 'handcuffs are on', and his head is rock steady.

Using the forearms as shock absorbers will take the pace off the ball.

Progression 1a (head-high shots)

Key points

(a)   Adopt the ready position.

(b)   Use forearms as shock absorbers to take the pace off the ball.

(c)   Spread fingers and thumbs to the side and behind the ball to form a 'W' shape.

(d)   Bring the ball back into the chest after the save.

(e)   Stand firm.

Progression 1b (ground shots)

The ball is rolled towards the keeper's feet from a distance of 6–10 yds (5.5–9 m). There are two methods of dealing with this type of shot and the goalkeeper must use the one he feels is more appropriate.

Using the long barrier method ensures that there is extra cover behind the hands.

In the scoop method it is essential that the legs are brought to less than ball-width apart.

(1) The long barrier method
Key points
(a) Adopt the ready position.
(b) Bend one knee forwards and turn the other leg sideways so that a long barrier is formed.
(c) Scoop the ball safely into the chest.

(2) The scoop method
Key points
(a) Adopt the ready position.
(b) Move the legs no less than the width of a ball.
(c) Bend at the hips and scoop the ball safely into the chest.

Practice 2 (feet and hands)

The keeper glides sideways to and fro across the surface.

Key points
(a) Glide with legs shoulder width apart and feet clipping the turf.
(b) Keep the hands in the ready position.

Progression 2a

From a distance of 6–10 yds (5.5–9 m) the ball is thrown at body height slightly to the side of the keeper.

Key points
(a) Adopt the ready position.
(b) Glide quickly into line of flight with feet shoulder width apart.
(c) Cup the ball into the body.

Progression 2b

The ball is thrown at head height to the side of the keeper from a distance of 6–10 yds (5.5–9 m).

Key points
(a) Adopt the ready position.
(b) Glide quickly into line of flight with feet shoulder width apart.

For waist-high shots the pace of the ball is absorbed in the midriff.

(c) Use arms as shock absorbers.
(d) Form a 'W' shape with the fingers and thumbs.
(e) Bring the ball into the chest.

Progression 2c

The ball is rolled slightly to the side of the keeper from a distance of 6–10 yds (5.5–9 m).

Key points
(a) Adopt the ready position.
(b) Glide quickly into the line of flight with feet shoulder width apart.
(c) Follow the long barrier or scoop technique.

Note: if the ball is moving quickly the slower long barrier method is unsuitable, so the scoop is recommended.

Progression 2d

The keeper has to glide zig-zag fashion through a series of markers. On reaching the last marker he then has to save a shot.

Key points
(a) Glide quickly with feet shoulder width apart.
(b) Lead with both hands as if wearing handcuffs.
(c) Keep the head steady.
(d) Be set in the ready position as the shot is struck.
(e) Use the appropriate handling technique.

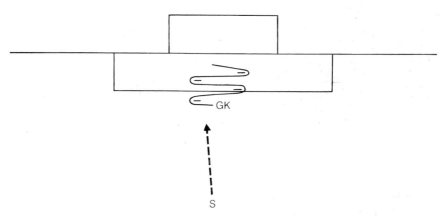

Zig-zag glide and save.

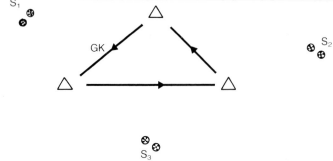

Move and save in the triangle.

Progression 2f

The keeper glides to and fro across his goal. As he moves towards one post the server will feed the ball in the other direction from a distance of 6–10 yds (5.5–9 m). The goalkeeper has to transfer his body-weight to make the save.

Key points
(a) Do not anticipate the save – glide quickly.
(b) Lead with the hands as if wearing handcuffs.
(c) Dig in and push off the foot furthest away from the ball.
(d) Remember: good handling.

When having to change direction rapidly it is important that the legs are not too wide apart so that 'spring' is not reduced.

When gliding across the goal the legs should be kept shoulder-width apart so that the ready position is maintained.

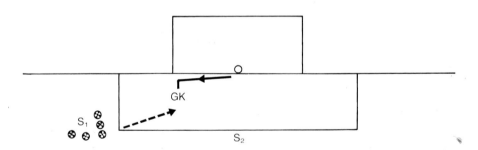

Glide across the goal and save the shot.

Progression 2h

The same as in 2g but another player stands on the six-yard line ready to finish any knock-downs from the keeper.

Key points
(a) – (f)   As in 2g.
(g)   If the cross shot cannot be gathered cleanly the ball should be deflected beyond the line of the far post.

Practice 3 (diving)

Many youngsters have a side on which they prefer to dive but the coach, by stripping the skill down, can diagnose the cause of this preference and rectify the weakness.

The goalkeeper sits on his haunches. The server, standing three yards away, feeds the ball to the side of the keeper who springs to catch the ball. Six repetitions for each side.

Key points
(a) Lead with the hands as if wearing handcuffs.
(b) Push hard off near leg.
(c) Remember: good handling.
(d) Land on shoulder and side (soft landings), *not* the elbows.

Progression 3a

As above but the keeper starts in a crouch position.

Progression 3b

As above but the keeper begins in a standing position.

Progression 3c

The goalkeeper starts in the middle of the goal. The server stands level with the post 6 yds (5.5 m) from the line. After bouncing the ball as a signal of his intention to throw, the server feeds the ball just inside the post. The goalkeeper has to spring to save. The service increases in difficulty as the keeper progresses. See the photograph on the next page.

Key points
(a) Adopt the ready position.
(b) Remember: quick feet (if necessary), good spring, good handling and soft landings (that is, on the shoulder and side).

For full-length saves it is important that the keeper lands on the softer, fleshy parts of his body.

Progression 3d (the collapsing save)

One of the most difficult saves that a keeper is faced with is the shot which passes quickly by his feet. His legs have to collapse away and he must lead with his hands because they can drop on the ball before the body can.

The goalkeeper stands in a goal 4–5 yds (3.5–4.5 m) in length. The server stands 6–8 yds (5.5–7 m) away and passes the ball to one side of the keeper. Having made the save the ball is returned to the server who passes to the other side. The keeper must be allowed to recover between saves.

Key points
(a) Adopt the ready position.
(b) React to the ball (that is, do not go down too early).
(c) Collapse the legs.
(d) Lead with both hands.
(e) Place the first hand behind the ball, the second on top.
(f) Pull the ball into the body.

This is an excellent practice for encouraging the keeper to lead with the hands and it certainly sharpens his reactions in dealing with the snap shot.

The collapsing save. The keeper's legs collapse under him.

He leads with both hands.

The first hand is behind the ball, and the second hand is on top.

The ball is pulled into the body and the knees come round to afford extra protection.

Deflecting the ball

The keeper should never attempt to use the fist to turn shots over the crossbar or round the post. The fist is uneven and is therefore an unreliable means of accurately deflecting the ball to safety, whereas using the fingers affords greater sensitivity and reach. If a shot is not going to be held the ball should be deflected for a corner or, at worst, outside the line of the posts. Parrying the ball straight back into play can have disastrous consequences. In order to achieve this type of deflection the wrist should be flicked as the ball makes contact with the fingers.

Practice 4 (turning the ball over the bar)

The keeper stands on the six-yard line with the server positioned on the penalty spot. The server feeds the ball over the keeper's head who has to back-pedal to catch or turn the ball to safety.

When turning the ball over the bar always use an open palm, because the fingers provide greater sensitivity and reach than a fist.

On a pitch measuring 20 yds (18 m) in length there are two goalkeepers in each goal. The object is to score in the opponents' goal using a throw, place-kick or volley. Each team may have an outfield player to capitalise on rebounds.

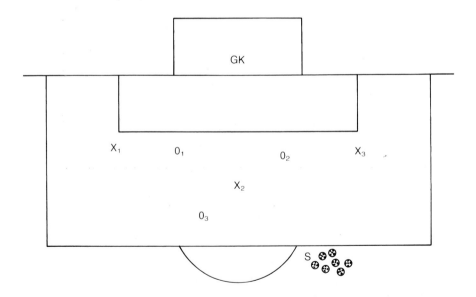

Quick-fire shot practice (see Practice 7 on next page).

Practice 7

This involves one goal and one keeper, with two teams of three players each. The pitch is defined by the lines of the penalty area. The coach feeds in balls from the outside and players of both teams are encouraged to shoot at the earliest opportunity.

Practice 8

This is a small-sided game using two goals and two keepers. The pitch is defined by the lines of the penalty area. The outfield players are encouraged to shoot at the earliest opportunity. The team which scores is rewarded with the next possession.

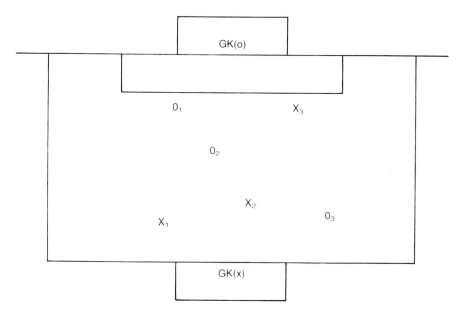

Small-sided game shooting practice.

Key points for practices 5, 6, 7 and 8
(a)   Adopt the ready position.
(b)   Remember: good feet, head steady and good handling.

unexpected because they will act instinctively anyway. However, if in training the coach can re-create these unpredictable situations the goalkeeper will know how to react when it happens again: and, who knows, it might be the save that turns the game.

Practice 1

The goalkeeper stands in the middle of his goal and does a forward roll. As he is getting to his feet the server shoots from 12–15 yds (11–13.75 m). The keeper makes the save.

Key points
(a) Take the weight on the shoulders.
(b) Come out of the roll in the ready position.
(c) Keep the head steady.
(d) Remember: good handling.

Practice 2

The goalkeeper faces his goal. On the command 'Turn!' the keeper spins round to save the shot from the server. The server varies his position and delivery.

Key points
(a)   Keep the head steady (eyes fixed on the ball).
(b)   Adopt the ready position.
(c)   Stay on the feet for as long as possible.
(d)   Be prepared to improvise.
(e)   Remember: good handling.

Practice 3

The goalkeeper sits on his six-yard line and the server stands near the edge of the penalty area. At the first signs of movement from the keeper the server chips the ball towards the goal. The keeper has to make the save.

Key points
(a)   Get up quickly.
(b)   Keep the head steady.
(c)   Take rapid mincing steps backwards.
(d)   Catch or deflect to safety.

Practice 4

The server starts with the ball wide on the edge of the penalty area and the keeper reacts to this position. The server then moves across the area to a marker at which he attempts to cut back the ball inside the near post. The practice is repeated from the other side of the area. As the keeper becomes more proficient the server can vary the timing and angle of the shot. See the diagram overleaf.

Key points
(a)   Get into line with the ball.
(b)   Glide with feet shoulder width apart.
(c)   Do not be pulled too far across the goal.
(d)   Get up the line if possible.
(e)   Be set in the ready position as the shot is struck.
(f)   Remember: good handling.

The cut back.

Practice 5

The keeper stands at one post facing out towards the touch-line. The server, standing 15–20 yds (13.75–18 m) from the goal-line, shouts 'Turn!' Once the keeper has spun round and is starting to cross his goal the server shoots for the empty corner. Repeat the practice from the other side of the goal.

Key points
(a) Look to get into line as quickly as possible.
(b) Glide rather than run.
(c) Keep the head steady.
(d) Get up the line if possible.
(e) Be prepared to improvise.

Practice 6 (deflections)

Four or five large heavy cones (of the motorway variety) are placed along the six-yard line. The server shoots from 18–20 yds (16.5–18 m) aiming to deflect the ball off the cones. The keeper has to save.

Using heavyweight cones can accustom the keeper to dealing with deflections.

Key points
(a) Adopt the ready position.
(b) Do not get too close to the cones (because it affords less reaction time).
(c) Keep the head steady.
(d) Go for the first shot but be ready to improvise if the ball is deflected.

Progression 6a

This practice is virtually the same as the previous one, but this time the cones are replaced by an outfield player who can make life difficult by obscuring the keeper's view and deflecting or dummying the ball. He will capitalise on any loose handling by the keeper. See the photograph overleaf.

Key points
(a) Adopt the ready position (keep calm and do not be distracted by nearby players).
(b) Do not get too close to the player in front.
(c) Keep the head steady.
(d) Go for the first shot but be ready to improvise if the ball is deflected.

Even though his view of the ball is obscured, the keeper should go for the first shot, but he should be ready to improvise in case the ball is deflected.

Practice 7 (saving with the feet)

Saving with the feet is no longer considered unorthodox and has been accepted as a skill in its own right. If the pace and closeness of the shot make safe handling impossible, the feet and legs are the next best barrier.

The keeper stands on his goal-line faced by ten balls placed along the six-yard box. There is a server at each end. The server at one end fires a ground shot straight at the keeper. As soon as he has saved with his feet, a shot arrives from the second server. This process continues until all of the balls have been kicked. The service must be rapid.

Key points
(a) Keep the head steady.
(b) Keep the legs less than a ball width apart.
(c) Turn the feet outwards to present a large barrier.
(d) Use little back lift.
(e) Deflect the ball to safety.

Progression 7a

As in Practice 7, but this time the service is varied so that the ball is not always delivered along the ground. The goalkeeper must decide to save either with the hands or feet.

Key points
(a) Keep the head steady.
(b) Adopt the ready position.
(c) Make good decisions (hands or feet).
(d) Apply the correct technique.

Practice 8 (long-distance shots)

Long-distance shots can often catch keepers out. This may be due to a lack of concentration or, more often, to a deceptively flighted shot. The goalkeeper must experience in training what it is like to face dipping, swerving and skidding shots.

The server occupies a position along the edge of the penalty area. Using volleys, half-volleys and ground shots he provides the keeper with a varied bombardment.

Key points
(a) Adopt the ready position.
(b) Get into line and up the line.
(c) Remember: good feet and good handling.
(d) Keep the head steady.

Progression 8a

This practice takes the form of a small-sided game (five against five plus two goalkeepers) in an area 40 yds × 40 yds (36.5 m × 36.5 m). Each team has three defenders and two attackers. Defenders must remain in their own half and attackers in their opponents'. The aim is for the defenders to create shooting opportunities for themselves. The attackers try to make life difficult for the opposition by dummying and deflecting shots.

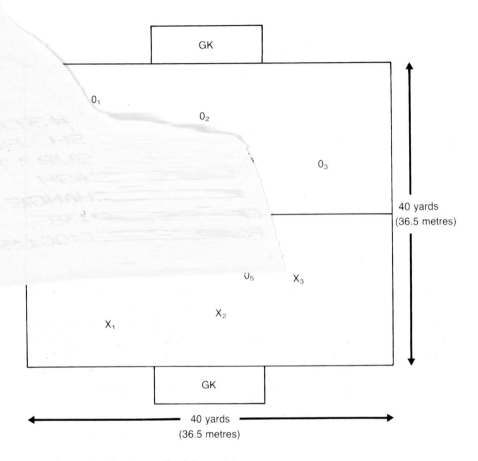

Long-distance shooting in a small-sided game.

Key points
(a) Adopt the ready position (expect a shot at any time).
(b) Get into line and up the line.
(c) Remember: good feet, good handling and good distribution.
(d) Keep the head steady.

5 Positioning

Making the difficult look easy is the secret of skilled performance. The goal-keeper who masters the art of positioning will make the job look simple. There are two basic movements involved in positioning:

(1) moving into line with the ball
(2) moving up the line towards the ball.

The angle and distance of the ball in relation to the goal will determine the keeper's position.

The keeper basically works in an arc where the size of the angle is proportional to the distance the goalkeeper has to come down the line. In other words, if the opponent's shooting angle is tight there is less need to narrow the angle. The whole point of positioning is to reduce the amount of goal shown to the shooter, so that if he is in a wide position his view of the goal is already diminished. The experienced keeper will narrow the angle quickly by cutting the diagonal (gliding into line and up the line in one movement).

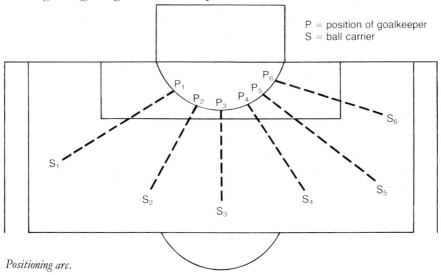

P = position of goalkeeper
S = ball carrier

Positioning arc.

47

By advancing down the line towards the ball the amount of goal shown to the striker is reduced.

The keeper should be constantly adjusting his position according to where the ball is. Even when play is in the opponents' half he should be in line with the ball and on the edge of his penalty area, ready to make a timely interception if the ball is played over the defence.

When the ball is in and around the penalty area it is important not to come too far down the line whilst the ball-carrier still has his head up. The skilful player will chip a keeper who commits himself in this way. It is safer to take the final steps forwards as the ball-carrier is preparing to shoot and has his eyes fixed on the ball. Finally, it is imperative that the keeper is set in the ready position as the shot is struck, because it is difficult to dive sideways whilst still moving forwards.

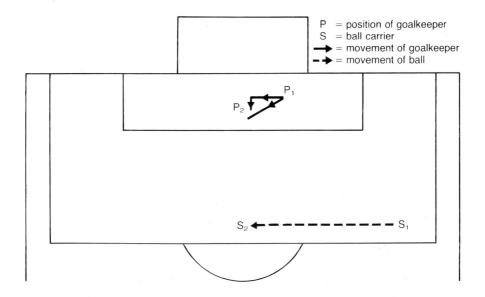

Cutting the diagonal, i.e. moving into and up the line in one movement.

Practice 1

The server moves with the ball along the edge of the penalty area and shoots. The keeper moves his feet in order to be in a position to save.

Key points
(a) Adopt a good starting position (for example, if the ball is 20 yds (18 m) out in a central position the keeper should be 3–6 yds (2.75–5.5 m) from his line).
(b) Move into line.
(c) Move up the line.
(d) Be set in the ready position when the shot is struck.
(e) Remember: good handling.

Progression 1a

Three heavyweight cones are bunched together on the edge of the penalty area. The server throws the ball at the cones and fires in the rebound. The keeper makes the save. Occasionally the ball may squeeze through the cones and the keeper must be ready to advance quickly to gather it. Using the cones as a rebounding surface leads to unpredictable shooting angles and therefore keeps the goalkeeper on his toes.

Key points
(a) Adopt a good starting position.
(b) Cut the diagonal (into the line/up the line).
(c) Steal extra forward steps as the shooter addresses the ball.
(d) Be set in the ready position as the shot is struck.
(e) Remember: good handling.

Practice 2

For this practice the server changes his position after every shot and always shoots on the move. The keeper faces the goal and turns on the command. The server waits for the keeper to pick up the line of the ball before shooting.

Key points
(a) Adopt a good starting position.
(b) Pick up the line of the ball quickly.
(c) Cut the diagonal.
(d) Be set in the ready position when the ball is struck.
(e) Remember: good handling.

Practice 3

Server 1 stands in a central position on the edge of the penalty area and passes the ball sideways so that server 2 may shoot. To force a quick shot, server 1 then pressurises server 2. The keeper has to save.

Key points
(a) Adopt a good starting position.
(b) Cut the diagonal.
(c) Steal extra steps forwards as the shooter addresses the ball.
(d) Be set in the ready position as the ball is struck.
(e) Remember: good handling.
(f) Be prepared to improvise if the shooter is close.

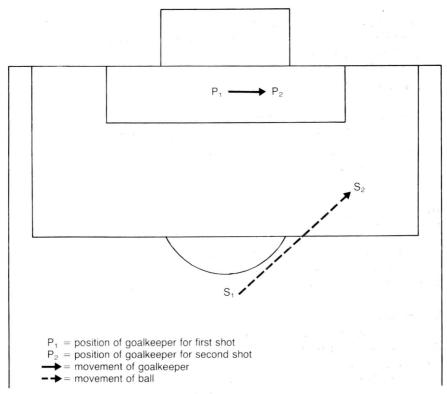

P₁ ———→ P₂

S₂

S₁

P$_1$ = position of goalkeeper for first shot
P$_2$ = position of goalkeeper for second shot
——→ = movement of goalkeeper
- -→ = movement of ball

Saving a shot after the ball has been passed sideways.

Practice 4

This practice takes the form of a small-sided game (two against two plus two goalkeepers) in an area 20 yds × 20 yds (18 m × 18 m). The outfield players may be limited to one or two touches to encourage them to shoot on sight. The goalkeeper has constantly to adjust his position in order to make the save.

Key points
(a) Always be ready for a shot.
(b) Adopt a good starting position.
(c) Cut the diagonal.
(d) Steal extra steps forwards as the shooter addresses the ball.
(e) Be set in the ready position as the ball is struck.
(f) Remember: good handling and good distribution.

6 Saving at an opponent's feet

Saving at an opponent's feet requires raw courage. However, if the technique is executed properly and with conviction, injury to the goalkeeper seldom results. Everyone expects a goal to be scored when a player is clear of the defence – that is, everyone except the keeper. It is essential that the keeper is mentally aggressive and is determined not to be beaten. If a goal is going to be conceded he must make the player earn his reward.

There are two stages involved in saving at an opponent's feet:

(a) decision making.
(b) application of the appropriate technique.

The keeper has to choose whether to rush the ball-carrier or to hold his ground. The decision to attack the ball must be based on the keeper's confidence in either winning possession outright or geting close enough to block the shot. Having assessed the situation and elected to attack the ball, he should move rapidly and positively. Any hesitation on his part can give the opponent the split second he needs to score. If the situation necessitates diving then the keeper should look to spread his body, thereby presenting the opponent with the widest barrier possible. Leading with the hands forces the keeper to spread himself in the desired manner, whilst advancing feet first reduces the size of the barrier.

If the opponent has good control of the ball, it is not recommended that the keeper attempts to rush him. By committing himself when there is little chance of winning possession or blocking the shot, the keeper will only succeed in making life easier for the ball-carrier. As the player approaches he is under pressure because a goal is expected, and he is further stressed by the numerous alternatives open to him. Does he take the ball round the keeper, attempt a chip, a side-foot or a blast? The keeper who rushes impetuously in this situation makes up the mind of the ball-carrier who will neatly side-step the rash lunge and put the ball in the net.

In all one against one situations in which the attacker has good possession the keeper must remember that time is on the side of the recovering defenders, so the longer he can stall the opponent the better. As the opponent approaches, the goalkeeper should advance cautiously, looking for any sign of miscontrol. If the forward does overrun the ball, the keeper should seize the opportunity to attack

When diving at player's feet be committed and lead with the hands to present the widest possible barrier.

and look to gather or at least to block the ball, using the body as a barrier. If the player has close control of the ball, the keeper must stay on his feet in an attempt to 'buy' himself time and better still to force his opponent wide so that the shooting angle is reduced. Recovering defenders should be encouraged to get across the path of the ball-carrier in order to reduce his options.

Forwards will try feinting moves in order to commit the keeper one way. He must ignore the body movements of his opponent and concentrate on the ball. Clever goalkeepers will even reverse the roles by pretending to attack the ball in order to distract the player.

Practice 1

Two players and one goalkeeper play in an area measuring 10 yds × 10 yds (9 m × 9 m). The players attempt to keep possession whilst the keeper aims either to claim the ball or to divert it out of the grid. The keeper is allowed to attack the ball after the first pass. After gaining five successes the goalkeeper rests.

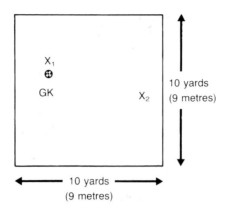

2 v 1 in a grid.

Key points
(a) Adopt a low ready position.
(b) Stay on the feet unless sure of winning the ball.
(c) Assess the situation, that is, look for any miscontrol.
(d) Threaten the ball-carrier.
(e) Try to manoeuvre the ball-carrier into a tight space (for example, a corner or on a line).
(f) Make a long barrier when diving.
(g) Be committed.

Progression 1a

In an area measuring 10 yds × 10 yds (9 m × 9 m) the ball-carrier has to score past the goalkeeper into a goal 4 yds (3.5 m) wide.

Key points
(a) Adopt a low ready position.
(b) Stay on the feet unless sure of winning the ball.
(c) Try to force the ball-carrier away from the goal.
(d) Attack if the player miscontrols the ball.
(e) Make a long barrier when diving.
(f) Do not foul.
(g) Be committed.

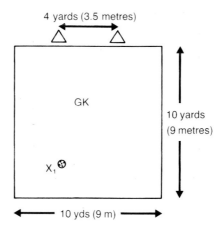

1 v 1, with a small goal inside the grid.

Progression 1b

The ball-carrier sets off 35 yds (32 m) from the goal with a defender following in pursuit from 40 yds (36.5 m). The goalkeeper and defender have to deal with the situation. The coach can vary the angle of approach.

Key points
(a) Adopt a good starting position (that is, advanced enough to inercept an overhit ball but not too far off the line to be susceptible to the chip).
(b) Come down the line cautiously.
(c) Assess the situation.
(d) Stay on the feet to 'buy' time.
(e) Threaten the ball.
(f) Try to force the opponent wide.
(g)   Make a long barrier when attacking the ball.
(h) Be prepared to save with the feet if the ball-carrier shoots early.
(i) Maintain good communication with the recovering defender.
(j) Be committed.

Progression 1c

The practice takes the form of a small-sided game (four against four including two goalkeepers) in an area measuring 60 yds × 40 yds (55 m × 36.5 m). For the

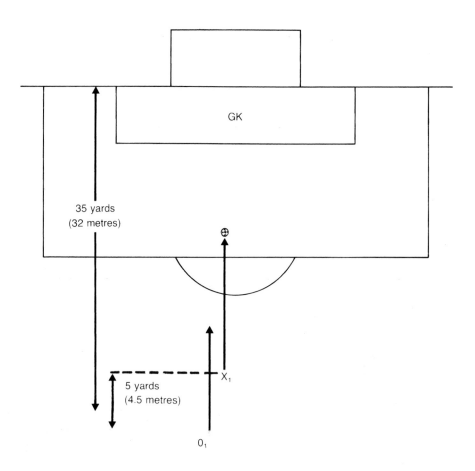

1 v 1 from the half-way line.

purposes of the practice the pitch is divided into three equal sections and out-field players are allowed only in the middle third of the pitch until the ball is played into one of the end zones. Only then may one player from each team enter the end zone. The aim of the practice is to give the keeper experience of realistic one against one situations.

Key points
(a) Adopt a good starting position.
(b) Be ready to intercept through balls.
(c) If the ball-carrier has control, 'buy' time and try to force him wide.
(d) When diving at feet, make a long barrier with the body.
(e) Be prepared to save close shots with the feet.
(f) Maintain good communication with the recovering defender.
(g) Be determined not to concede a goal.

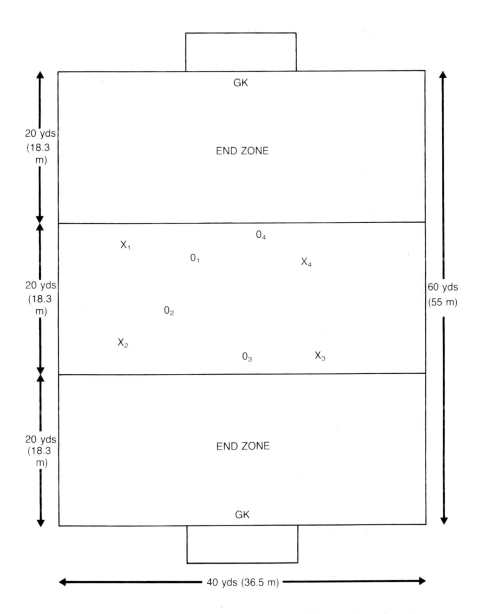

Small-sided game, which requires sound decision making and good technique from the goalkeeper.

7 The high cross

This is without doubt the most difficult aspect of goalkeeping since it requires crucial decision making and the application of good technique under varying degrees of pressure. As a large percentage of goals result from high balls played into the penalty area, a keeper's worth is often measured in terms of his ability to deal effectively with crosses.

Goalkeepers who consistently come to gather crosses are always very popular with their team-mates. However, the easy option is to remain on the goalline and rely on either the defenders' ability to clear the danger or a last ditch reaction save. This reluctance to leave the line to gather crosses is usually due to a lack of confidence on the keeper's part. Perhaps his previous attempts to deal with high balls have been unsuccessful and this has led to the development of a negative attitude.

Nevertheless, the keeper must realise that he has a responsibility to use the advantage that the laws of the game allow him in order to assist his team-mates in repelling the attack. Of course there will be the odd error of judgement or days when conditions are not conducive to good handling and the keeper will be praying for the ball to burst rather than have it crossed into the goal-mouth. However, he must be mentally tough and demonstrate complete faith in his ability to deal effectively with the situation. On those occasions when confidence is low he must convince himself that as he has taken crosses in the past he can do it again. Furthermore, a shaky, hesitant goalkeeper who prefers to stay on his line will unsettle defenders and inspire opponents.

Stages in handling crosses

Starting position

When the ball is wide and about to be crossed, the goalkeeper's starting position is crucial since a yard either way can mean the difference between being close enough to attack the ball or being out of range. If the ball is wide, the keeper should start from a position slightly behind the centre of the goal. The reason for this is that it is easier to take the ball moving forwards than backwards. A

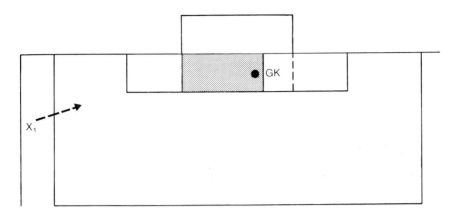

Good starting position. When the ball is wide, the goalkeeper's position should be back from the centre of the goal. Most of the keeper's work will be done while moving forwards (see shaded area).

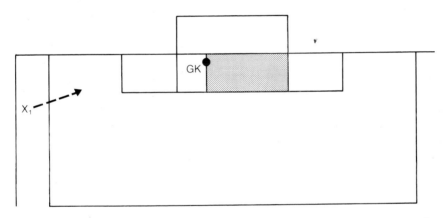

Poor starting position. Adopting a position too close to the near post will present the keeper with problems if the ball is played beyond him. It is easier to take the ball when moving forwards than when going backwards.

keeper starting too close to the near post will be struggling to deal with a deep cross. As the ball-carrier nears the goal the keeper should move towards his near post to cover a possible shot.

Depending on how near the crosser is, the keeper should be a yard or two off the goal-line. If the ball is played 6–8 yds (5.5–7.25 m) from the goal, the keeper, due to his advanced starting position, will still be able to reach it.

The ideal starting position for a high cross is in the rear of the goal and a yard or so from the line. Note the sideways stance.

Regarding the keeper's stance, I would recommend an open body position as if he were preparing to sprint to the crosser. In this position he is ready to make a rapid movement forwards and is also facing the play if the cross is whipped in out of catching range.

Assessing the flight of the ball

Although it sounds obvious, the goalkeeper must assess the flight of the ball before moving. The many distractions around him, such as his defenders, his opponents and his own expectations of where he feels the ball will be played, will tempt him to anticipate the cross. This type of gambling can prove disastrous. The clever winger will vary the length of his crosses, so the keeper cannot afford to sell himself before the ball is kicked.

Generally speaking, for crosses that are driven in the keeper must move fast and win the race to the ball. For crosses floated in he must arrive late so that he is not caught underneath the ball. By making his attack at the last possible moment he will be able to use a running jump, and as he will be aware of the players challenging him his decision to catch or punch will be more reliable.

Decision-making

Having assessed the flight of the ball, the keeper must elect either to stay on his line or to attack the ball. This decision is based on the ball's trajectory, pace and distance from the goal-line, as well as the proximity of other players. If, in the keeper's judgement, he can deal effectively with the situation then he should come for the cross. When circumstances militate against safe handling of the cross the decision should be to stay put.

Once he has decided not to go for the cross, the keeper should remain on his line instead of being drawn to the ball. By stepping back to the line the keeper might buy himself that extra split second in which to make a reaction save. In allowing himself to be drawn to the ball the keeper would be caught in 'no man's land', and would be vulnerable to the looping header beyond him.

After electing to come for the cross it is essential that the keeper makes contact with the ball. From the time he decides to go for the cross his intention must be to catch the ball because that will effectively end the attack. However, at the last moment he must re-appraise the situation and decide whether to catch, punch or deflect the ball. This decision is based on how confident the keeper is of making a safe catch.

If the pressure from opponents between the keeper and the ball makes safe handling unlikely, then the keeper should attempt to punch the ball. When the ball is swinging in towards the crossbar and catching would be difficult, the keeper should deflect over the bar for a corner. Similarly, if the goalkeeper is back-pedalling beyond the back post and cannot reach the ball with two hands, he should palm the ball to safety.

It is often said that any ball played into the six-yard box should be the keeper's responsibility. This is not always the case because sometimes defenders are better positioned to clear the ball. This is particularly true for those crosses driven in at head height or below. Here the keeper should prepare himself for a sharp reaction save.

Conversely, the space beyond the six-yard line should not be regarded as a 'no go area' for the keeper. The good keeper may find himself 7–8 yds (6.5–7.25 m)

The keeper should decide to gather the ball if he is confident of making a clean catch.

If the position of other players makes a safe catch unlikely, the keeper should elect to punch.

from his line taking a high hanging cross. Time and safety factors determine whether the keeper should come for the cross.

Communication

One way in which the keeper can create space for himself to collect the cross is by the use of his voice. If the ball is wide but fairly deep, the goalkeeper will make life difficult for himself by allowing his defenders to drop deep around the six-yard line. That serves only to encourage attackers to move nearer to the goal. By instructing his defenders to hold their line at, for example, the penalty spot opponents will be discouraged from making runs into the danger area. Those who do so before the ball is kicked will be off side. If the defenders leave this space and the cross is played in, the keeper will have both the room and the time to collect the ball under minimal pressure. When the winger progresses towards the by-line the goalkeeper should instruct his defenders to stay level since opponents will be off side if they move ahead of the ball.

The keeper should communicate with his defenders every time that the ball is played into the penalty area (*see* Chapter 9). As far as crosses are concerned, if the keeper decides to come he should call 'Keeper's!' and if he elects to stay he should call 'Away!' The way in which the keeper communicates is important. His calls must be loud, clear and positive. Defenders will be unsettled by hesitant or panicky instructions. The keeper must give the impression that he is calm and in control of the situation. A good, confident call is often the prelude to a good, confident catch. A keeper who exudes confidence will inspire and set the tone for the rest of the defence.

Technique

Having assessed the flight, decided to come for the cross and then communicated his intention to team-mates, the keeper must look to gather the ball at the highest possible point. By not attacking the ball there is a danger of opponents getting to it first. Some goalkeepers make the mistake of moving perpendicularly from the line to catch a cross instead of moving diagonally into the flight of the ball to take it earlier and at the highest possible point.

With the benefit of a good starting position more often than not the keeper will take the cross moving forwards. He should take off on one foot, bringing up the other leg to give extra lift and some protection against opponents' challenges. If a cross is a deep one, the keeper should move backwards quickly using little mincing steps before taking off from one foot.

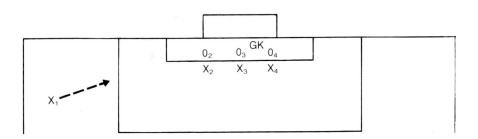

By allowing defenders to drop into deep positions the keeper will invite opponents into advanced positions and will thus create problems.

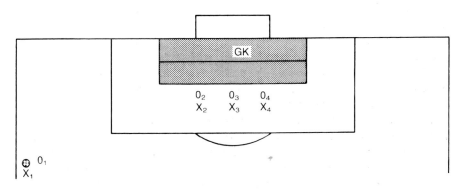

By pushing defenders up, the goalkeeper will create space for himself (see shaded area) in which he can attack the ball under minimal pressure.

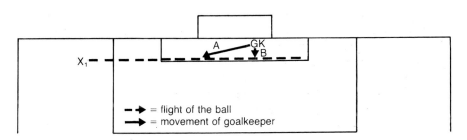

Attacking the ball. Movement A is preferable to movement B because it results in the ball being taken earlier.

Catching

It is recommended that the goalkeeper makes his catch in front of the line of the body and not directly above his head. There are several good reasons for this:

(a) it allows him to see the ball into his hands
(b) by using his arms as shock absorbers it provides some margin for error if any mishandling occurs
(c) it offers greater leverage if at the last moment he decides to punch.

It goes without saying that a catch is preferable to a punch, but the keeper must weigh up the risk factor and choose the safer option.

Punching

If the decision is to punch, then the keeper must aim for height and distance. Added together, these two factors give defenders time to deal with the next wave of the attack. Ideally, the keeper should look to punch the ball out of the danger area. For those balls moving towards the keeper a punch should be made with two hands as this makes for a more reliable contact. Although using one fist will give greater reach and may be necessary in emergencies, it can result in a

The keeper should use one fist when punching the ball across the line of flight.

When gathering a high cross the keeper should take off from one foot and use the forearms as shock absorbers so that the ball is taken in front of his body.

For a double-fisted punch the knuckles must not be clenched too tightly and the wrists should be kept rigid.

mishit punch because the striking surface is narrow and often the keeper is hitting the ball across the body. One-handed punches are more appropriate than the double-fisted clearance when the ball is moving away from the keeper.

In order to achieve maximum height and distance in his punch the keeper should use the flat part of the fist and strike through the bottom half of the ball. The movement should be more of a jab than a swing. He should avoid clenching the fist too tightly as this makes the striking surface uneven and will result in a mistimed punch. The wrists should stay rigid throughout.

Deflecting

If the ball is swinging in dangerously close to the crossbar and a safe catch is unlikely, the keeper should attempt to turn the ball over the bar using the open palm of the hand furthest from the goal-line. An open palm affords greater reach

The keeper should use the arm furthest away from the goal-line to turn over the ball passing dangerously close to the cross-bar.

than a fist and the fingers are more sensitive than knuckles. Using the arm furthest away from the goal-line allows the keeper greater reach and is more comfortable as the wrist rotates forwards rather than backwards.

The same technique is recommended if the keeper is back-pedalling beyond the back post and is unable to catch the ball. The ball should be deflected over the by-line for a corner.

As collecting a high cross is an advanced skill, coaches should not expect perfect catches from young boys and girls. Most children below the age of 13 do not possess the hand size or strength to catch a high ball. Therefore, it is quite acceptable for goalkeepers of that age to parry the ball first and to follow up quickly with a secondary save.

Practice 1 (catching a high ball moving forwards)

From a distance of 10 yds (9 m) the server throws the ball high into the air so that the keeper moves forwards to catch it.

Key points
(a)   Adopt the ready position.
(b)   Assess the flight of the ball.
(c)   Take off on one foot.
(d)   Take the ball at the higher point so that it is in front of the eye line (using the forearms as shock absorbers).
(e)   Remember: good handling (bring the ball back into the chest).

Progression 1a (catching a high ball moving backwards)

From a distance of 6 yds (5.5 m) the server feeds the ball over the keeper's head so that he has to move quickly backwards to make the catch.

Key points
(a)   Adopt the ready position.
(b)   Assess the flight.
(c)   Take quick, mincing steps backwards.
(d)   Take off on one foot.
(e)   Catch the ball at the highest point so that it is in front of the eye line (using the forearms as shock absorbers).

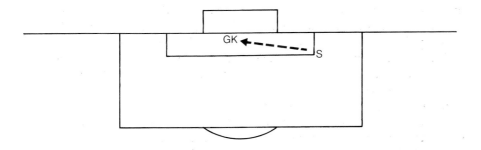

Catching the ball from the side.

(f) Remember: good handling (bring the ball back into the chest).
(g) Go to ground if off balance.

Progression 1c (catching a ball delivered from the side)

The server stands at the junction of the six-yard box and throws the ball across the face of the goal. The service is varied so that the keeper takes some balls going forwards and others going backwards. See diagram above.

Key points
(a) Adopt a good starting position (backwards from centre).
(b) Take up sideways stance.
(c) Assess the flight of the ball.
(d) Take off on one foot.
(e) Take the ball at the highest point (using the forearms as shock absorbers).
(f) Remember: good handling (bring the ball back into the chest).

Progression 1d (catching a cross without opposition)

Having dealt effectively with hand service it is now appropriate to move to a more realistic practice where crosses are kicked in. The novice keeper will initially experience problems because catching crosses is much more difficult than dealing with thrown balls.

The server crosses the ball from a wide position and the keeper comes to collect the cross.

Key points

(a) Adopt a good starting position (backwards from centre and one or two yards from the goal-line).
(b) Take up a sideways stance.
(c) Assess the flight.
(d) Take off on one foot.
(e) Take the ball at the highest point (using the forearms as shock absorbers).
(f) Good handling (bring the ball back into the chest).

Progression 1e (taking crosses with a defender in attendance)

As in 1d, but a defender is introduced.

Key points

(a) Adopt a good starting position (backwards from centre).
(b) Take up a sideways stance.
(c) Assess the flight.
(d) Decide whether to collect or stay on your line.
(e) Communicate: call 'Keeper's!' or 'Away!'
(f) If staying, get back on your line. If coming, take the ball at the highest point using a one-footed take-off.

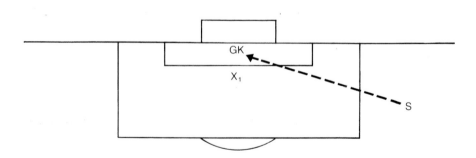

Catching the ball with the help of a defender.

(g) Use arms as shock absorbers.
(h) Remember: good handling (bring the ball back into the chest).
(i) Defender covers on the line if the keeper comes to collect.

Progression 1f (from hand service taking a high ball under pressure)

As for progression 1c, but an opponent stands in the ball's line of flight. The server varies the trajectory and pace of the ball so that the keeper has to decide whether to catch or punch.

Key points
(a) Adopt a good starting position (backwards from centre).
(b) Take up a sideways stance.
(c) Assess the flight (react to the ball, not to the movement of the opponent).
(d) Take off from one foot to take the ball at the highest point.
(e) If the trajectory is low, win the race to the ball. If the ball is hung up, go late.
(f) Decide whether to catch or punch.
(g) Make sure you handle well if you decide to catch. Aim for height and distance if you decide to punch.

Progression 1g (taking a cross with two defenders and one attacker)

The server crosses from a wide position but is encouraged to vary the angle of the delivery. The keeper is assisted by two defenders and opposed by one attacker.

Key points
(a) Adopt a good starting position (backwards from centre and one or two yards off the line.
(b) Take up a sideways stance.
(c) Do not allow defenders to drop too deep unless the crosser is close to the by-line.
(d) Assess the flight.
(e) Decide whether to come for the ball or stay on your line.
(f) If you decide to come, shout 'Keeper's!' and if you elect to stay, shout 'Away!'

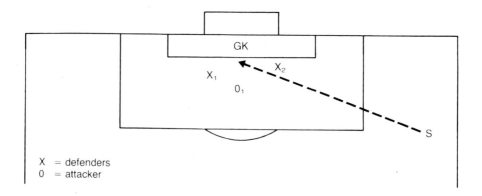

Catching the ball, with two defenders and one attacker taking part in the practice.

(g) If you come for the ball, take it at the highest point. If you stay on your line, move back to the line and prepare for a shot or a header.

(h) Decide whether to catch or punch.

(i) Remember: good handling and good punching.

Progression 1h (small-sided crossing game)

The practice takes the form of a small-sided game (five against five plus two goalkeepers) in an area 50 yds × 50 yds (36.5 m × 45.75 m). Each team has a right-winger (x5 and o5) who is allowed to move unchallenged up and down a 5-yds (4.5-m) channel. The goalkeeper, or outfield player, passes the ball to the winger who makes ground before crossing into the opponents' goal-mouth. Off sides apply. See diagram on next page.

Key points

(a) Adopt a good starting position.

(b) Remember: good communication, good decisions, good technique (catching or punching) and good distribution.

Practice 2 (deflecting crosses to safety)

The goalkeeper positions himself ready for a cross. The server, standing at the junction of the six-yard box and the by-line, throws the ball towards the crossbar.

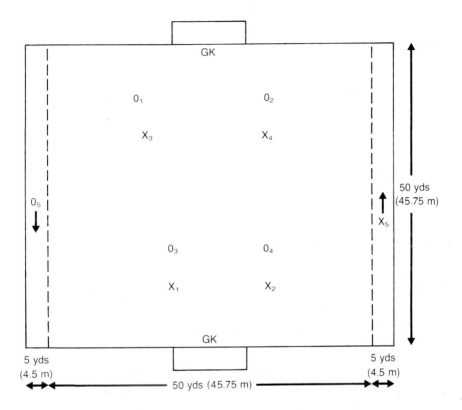

Small-sided game to practise taking crosses.

Key points
(a)   Adopt a good starting position.
(b)   Take up a sideways stance.
(c)   Assess the flight.
(d)   Decide whether to catch or deflect the ball over the bar.
(e)   To palm over use the hand furthest away from the goal-line.

Practice 3 (punching)

The goalkeeper sits facing the server who feeds the ball from a distance of two or three yards to the keeper's right hand. He punches the ball back, aiming for the server's chest. The keeper punches ten times with the right hand, ten times with the left hand and ten times with both.

75

Key points
(a) Keep the wrist rigid.
(b) Make contact with the flat part of the fist.
(c) Jab straight through the bottom half of the ball.
(d) Follow straight through.

Progression 3a

The goalkeeper lies in the prone position facing the server who positions himself a yard away. The server feeds the ball to the keeper's right hand and he punches the ball back. The goalkeeper looks to achieve as much height as possible in the punch. The serving schedule is the same as for practice 3.

Key points
As in practice 3.

For best results when punching jab through the bottom half of the ball.

Progression 3b

This practice seeks to give the goalkeeper the experience of punching when he is not ideally positioned.

The goalkeeper sits facing the server who, from a distance of three or four yards, feeds the ball well to the right-hand side. The keeper has to roll over and punch the ball back over the server's head. The exercise is repeated ten times for each side.

Key points
(a)   Roll over on to the shoulder.
(b)   Keep the wrist rigid.
(c)   Jab straight through the bottom half of the ball.
(d)   Follow straight through, looking for height and distance.

8 Distribution

If the goalkeeper is the last line of defence he is, by implication, the first line of attack. For this reason it is imperative that he distributes the ball well. It is infuriating to see a keeper, having made a fine catch, surrender possession through a careless throw or kick.

The manner in which the coach instructs his goalkeeper to distribute the ball will form the basis for the team's pattern of play. Some coaches will encourage their goalkeeper to throw the ball at every opportunity so that play can be built up from the back. Others will prefer their keepers to miss out the defence and midfield by kicking deep into enemy territory in order to maximise his own team's strengths and/or to exploit the individual weaknesses of his opponents.

With such a heavy responsibility the goalkeeper should constantly practise throwing and kicking techniques so that his distribution becomes an asset to the team and not a liability. Since he has to take more free kicks (off sides and goal-kicks mostly) than any other player, it is essential that he is one of the most proficient dead-ball kickers in the team. It is not sufficient to be able to kick the ball over a great distance – he must do it accurately and consistently. If the keeper is reliable with his kicks, the team can then adapt their tactics accordingly. However, if a goalkeeper's distribution is erratic, his kicking will take on a negative rather than a positive association.

Generally speaking, throws are quicker and more accurate than kicks and the keeper will use them to guarantee his team possession. It is important, therefore, that a ball thrown by the goalkeeper does not give the recipient a control problem. If the receiving player has to waste precious seconds in controlling the ball, it defeats the whole object of the exercise.

Having mastered the techniques of throwing, dead-ball kicking and volleying, the keeper must develop an understanding of when and where to use them. As soon as the goalkeeper collects the ball he should scan the whole pitch, looking for an opportunity to make a penetrative pass or to change the direction of play. He should only distribute quickly when the intended receiver is in a position to worry the opposition.

For example, if the keeper notices that the opposition, in pushing forwards, have not left any covering defenders at the back, he should risk a quick kick. Similarly, when receiving the ball from one side of the pitch the keeper should always glance to the opposite flank because there is a strong possibility that a team-mate will be in space. A quick throw might catch the opposition (who were attacking down the other side of the field) on the hop. On a cautionary note, however, the goalkeeper should not be thinking about the throw before making the save. Many keepers have been embarrassed because they have taken their eye off the ball at the last moment.

Sometimes the state of play will dictate how the keeper distributes. If his team is under severe pressure the goalkeeper should take the heat out of the situation by taking his time when in possession. He should also be able to assess the strengths and weaknesses of the opposition and distribute the ball accordingly. For instance, it would be futile persisting with high clearances when his own forwards are dwarfed by the opposing defenders. As all opponents are different and pose varying problems and challenges, it is important that teams are adaptable as far as receiving the ball from the goalkeeper is concerned. Coaches who neglect working on distribution from the keeper do so at their peril.

Throwing techniques

The roll

The roll is used for very short distances, usually to distribute to defenders on the edge of the penalty area. The keeper must never roll the ball to a team-mate standing in the penalty area because he is not allowed to pick up a return pass. The actual technique is similar to the ten pin bowling action where the ball is kept in contact with the ground for as long as possible. The keeper can achieve this by keeping low and following through on the roll.

The javelin throw

This is used for slightly longer distances and involves a whiplash action which resembles throwing a javelin. By flicking the wrist on delivery, slice will be imparted to the ball, thus keeping the bounce low. The risk of giving the receiver a difficult bouncing ball will be further reduced if the keeper stays low throughout the delivery. Ideally, the ball should reach the recipient below knee height.

The overarm throw

If performed well and employed at the appropriate moment, this throw can be a potent attacking weapon because it can play several opponents out of the game at one time. It is used to cover distances beyond which the keeper would have to

The roll is used for very short distances and is similar to a ten pin bowling action.

(Right) The javelin throw is used to cover distances between 10–20 yds (9–18 m). Imparting slice on the ball will keep the bounce low, making control easy.

The overarm throw is most effective when it is used to change the direction of attack. The point of release will determine the amount of time the ball spends in the air.

kick. It is often employed when the opposition have committed numbers in attack and the goalkeeper tries to catch them on the break. These throws are more effective when kept low because they take less time to reach their intended target. However, when oponents are blocking the direct route the ball has to spend most of its journey airborne.

The actual technique is a bowling action where the goalkeeper takes the ball back with a fairly straight arm and follows through quite vigorously. The point of release depends upon how much 'air' the keeper intends to give the ball. If he is looking to clear players, then an early release is recommended, but if there are no obstacles between himself and his target not only can he release the ball late but can also impart slice in order to keep it low.

Kicking techniques

The place kick

Goalkeepers who consistently achieve distance and accuracy from their dead-ball kicks will prove an asset to their team. It is demoralising for a team to be regularly put on the defensive by its keeper's weak place-kicking. However, even though he fails to clear any great distance the keeper can save the day if he can kick accurately to strategically placed team-mates. The coach should be aware of his goalkeeper's strengths and weaknesses in this department and should implement an appropriate pattern of play. If the keeper consistently kicks long, he can push players well forward into the opponents' half since players cannot be off side from a goal-kick. But if the keeper repeatedly fails to reach the half-way line, the target players can drop deeper in order to win the vital first touch.

Coaches of school teams should persevere with their goalkeepers even if their goal-kicks are poor. Players at school level are at a crucial stage of their development and should not be denied learning experiences such as taking goal-kicks. Moreover, having an outfield player taking goal-kicks encourages the opponents' strikers to push forward in the knowledge that they will not be off side if the ball is returned by their defence.

Regardless of whether or not the keeper is a good dead-ball kicker, he must never aim across the field. If the kick falls short, he will be caught out of position with very little time to do anything about it. To be safe he should always aim his kicks to the same side of the field.

The volley

The volley is the more common method used when kicking from the hands. The advantages of the volley are that the ball can be passed over considerable distances and it is fairly reliable.

The half-volley

If executed well the half-volley is a more effective technique than the volley because its lower trajectory results in the ball reaching the target in a shorter time. It is useful when playing into a strong wind or when there is an opportunity for a quick counter-attack. However, care must be taken when playing on muddy or bumpy grounds because good contact with the ball cannot be guaranteed. With this in mind the technique should never be attempted in the six-yard area.

Practice 1 – the roll

The keeper rolls the ball to a receiver standing 6–10 yds (5–9 m) away. The receiver controls and then returns the ball.

Key points
(a)   Point the leading foot in the direction of the target.
(b)   Use a ten pin bowling action.
(c)   Keep low.
(d)   Ensure a good follow-through.
(e)   Do not cause the receiver problems with control – keep the ball low.

Progression 1a

As in practice 1, but on the command the receiver sets off at an angle and the keeper has to find him with a rolled pass.

Key points
(a)   Point the front foot in the direction of the target.
(b)   Keep low.
(c)   Ensure a good follow-through.
(d)   Aim slightly in front of the receiver so that he does not have to check his stride.
(e)   Keep the ball low so that the receiver does not have a control problem.

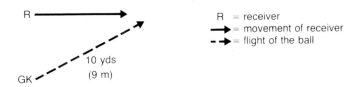

Defender receiving a throw on the run.

Practice 2 – the javelin throw

The keeper uses the javelin throw to pass to a receiver standing 10–15 yds (9–14 m) away. The receiver controls and then returns the ball.

Key points
(a) Point the front foot and non-throwing arm in the direction of the target.
(b) Keep low.
(c) Use a javelin arm action.
(d) Flick the wrist on delivery to impart slice on the ball.
(e) Keep the ball low (do not give the receiver a control problem).

Progression 2a

As for practice 2, but on the command the receiver sets off at an angle and the keeper has to pass to him using a javelin throw.

Key points
(a) Point the front foot and non-throwing arm in the direction of the target.
(b) Keep low.
(c) Use a javelin arm action.
(d) Flick the wrist on delivery to impart slice to the ball.
(e) Aim slightly in front of the receiver so that he does not have to check his stride.
(f) Keep the ball low so that it does not present a control problem for the receiver.

Practice 3 – the overarm throw

The keeper throws the ball using the overarm technique to a target 15–35 yds (13.75–32 m) away. The receiver controls and then returns the ball.

Key points
(a) Point the leading foot and non-throwing arm towards the target.
(b) Ensure a straight arm preparation.
(c) Use a vigorous follow-through and a late release.
(d) Flick your wrist on delivery to impart slice to the ball.
(e) Keep the ball low so that the receiver is not presented with a control problem.

Progression 3a

As in practice 3, but an opponent stands in the line of flight so that the keeper has to clear him to find his target.

Key points
(a) Point the leading foot and non-throwing arm towards the target.
(b) Ensure a straight arm preparation.
(c) Use a vigorous follow-through with an early release.
(d) Aim to drop the ball at the receiver's feet.

Progression 3b

As in practice 3, but the receiver sets off at an angle and the keeper has to pass to him using the overarm technique.

Key points
(a) Point your leading foot and non-throwing arm towards the target.
(b) Ensure a straight arm preparation.
(c) Use a vigorous follow-through with a late release.
(d) Flick the wrist on delivery to impart slice to the ball.
(e) Aim slightly in front of the receiver so that he does not have to check his stride.
(f) Keep the ball low so that the receiver is not presented with a control problem.

Progression 3c

As in progression 3a, but the receiver sets off at an angle and the keeper has to by-pass the intruding player to find his target.

Key points
(a) Point your leading foot and non-throwing arm towards the target.
(b) Ensure a straight arm preparation.
(c) Use a vigorous follow-through with an early release.
(d) Aim to drop the ball at the receiver's feet so that he does not have to check his stride.

Practice 4 – the place kick

The keeper takes a goal-kick, aiming to hit a target 10 yds (9 m) wide on the half-way line.

Key points
(a) Make an angled approach.
(b) The non-kicking foot should be positioned about 12 in (30 cm) to the side of the ball and behind it.

Wide-angled approach on a dead ball kick, with the foot striking through the bottom half of the ball.

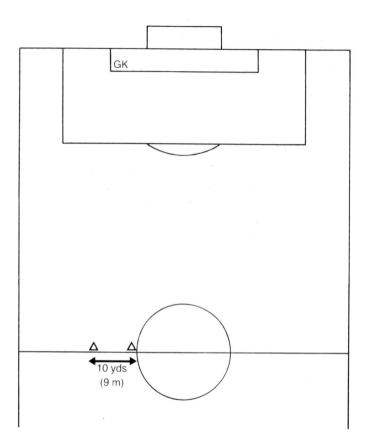

Goal-kick practice.

(c) The kicking foot should be pointed outwards, with the ankle firm and extended.

(d) Contact should be made with the instep through the bottom half of the ball.

(e) The eyes should be looking down at the ball and the head should be kept steady.

When kicking into a strong wind the keeper should aim for a lower trajectory by reducing the angle of approach and planting the non-kicking foot closer to the ball.

Practice 5 – the volley

The keeper volleys the ball over four 10-yard (9 m) grids so that the receiver catches it at chest height.

Key points
(a) Hold the ball out in front of the body at waist height.
(b) Drop the ball on to the kicking foot.
(c) Using the instep, strike the ball in front of the body.
(d) Place the non-kicking foot behind the line of the ball.
(e) Make contact through the middle of the ball.
(f) Aim for a smooth follow-through.
(g) Keep the head straight, with the eyes fixed on the ball.

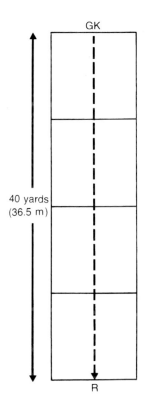

Volley practice.

89

The volley: the ball is held out in front of the body at waist height and is then dropped.

The non-kicking foot is planted behind the ball. The head is kept steady throughout.

Contact is made with the instep through the bottom half of the ball.

A half volley can reach its target quicker than a volley can. It is particularly useful when kicking into a strong wind.

Progression 5a

The organisation is the same as in practice 4 except that the keeper volleys to a target placed on the half-way line (the distance may be varied according to ability). Points are awarded for an accurate volley so that progress may be monitored.

Key points
As for practice 5.

Practice 6 – the half-volley

As for practice 5 but the goalkeeper half-volleys the ball to the receiver.

Key points
(a) Hold the ball out in front of the body at waist height.
(b) Drop the ball so that it pitches just in front of the non-kicking foot.
(c) Follow through with the instep of the kicking foot, striking through the bottom half of the ball.
(d) Follow through with the body leaning backwards.
(e) Keep the head steady, with the eyes fixed on the ball.

To achieve a lower trajectory the ball should be dropped closer to the non-kicking foot and contact should be made through the centre of the ball. The body should be leaning forwards on the follow-through.

9   Supporting the defence

There is more to goalkeeping than being directly involved in the action. As the last line of the defensive unit, the goalkeeper should not only be prepared to act as a sweeper if the ball is played over his defenders but also as a passing option if his team has possession. Quick thinking and astute positioning can diffuse potentially dangerous situations. Allied to this positional responsibility is the worth of the goalkeeper as a source of ongoing information. After all, he does enjoy a view of the whole pitch and is therefore perfectly placed to direct defensive operations.

Supporting position

The distance the goalkeeper should be from his own goal-line varies according to the proximity of the ball. The following table may be used as a guide.

Location of the ball	Keeper's distance from the goal-line
(i) in the opposite penalty area	18 yds (16.5 m)
(ii) between the opposite penalty area and half-way line	12–18 yds (11–16.5 m)
(iii) between the half-way line and the arc of the centre circle	6–12 yds (5.5–11 m)
(iv) between the arc of the centre circle and the edge of the penalty area.	3–6 yds (2.75–5.5 m)

Except when the ball is in a wide (and unlikely crossing) position, the goal-keeper should follow the basic principles and get into line. If the keeper maintains the optimum angle and distance, he will be ideally placed to intercept through balls and assist defenders with back passes.

One of the qualities all good defences possess is compactness, and the keeper should ensure that he does not become too detached from the rear-most defender. Skilful opponents will exploit large spaces left at the back of defences, so the goalkeeper should be aware of his sweeping role as play moves towards his goal. If the opponents do play a through ball, the well positioned keeper will be able to select the safest option from the following:

(a)   leave the area and kick the ball to safety (preferably into touch)
(b)   wait until the ball reaches the penalty area and collect it
(c)   allow defenders to affect a clearance or make a back pass.

Each of these options must be accompanied by an appropriate call.

If the keeper allows defenders to make a back pass he must take up a position that gives the passer some margin of error. A harassed defender would rather pass over six yards than one or two, so the goalkeeper must retreat to make the passing distance more appealing. The goalkeeper must be prepared for the misdirected pass and not wander too far from the line of his posts. If the back pass is wayward, let it be at the expense of a corner and not an own goal.

Communication

Goalkeepers who communicate well with defenders are much valued. Clear, early calls can alert team-mates to hitherto unseen dangers as well as averting any confusion arising between players. Furthermore, constant communication with his defenders will aid the keeper's concentration, especially during those periods in the game when he is largely inactive.

It is important that the goalkeeper knows what, how and when to communicate. As he is in the privileged position of seeing the whole pitch, the keeper can alert defenders to blind-side runs from opponents. As play develops down one flank a quick glance across the pitch might reveal unmarked players. An early call to a team-mate can ensure that the unmarked player is picked up. The goalkeeper must be specific in the information he directs at the team-mate who is dealing with the situation. In this case it may be 'John, pick up the spare man at the back post!'

If the ball is played over the defence, the keeper must make his intentions clear in order to avoid any confusion. Any hesitation on the part of the keeper and his defenders could have disastrous consequences. If the keeper intends to claim the ball, he must call 'Keeper's ball, let it run!' On no account should the defender play the ball if the goalkeeper is coming to collect it. When he wants the defender to make a back pass he should shout 'Keeper's on. Push it back!' Merely to call 'Keeper's!' does not clarify the situation sufficiently. The call should leave the defenders in no doubt as to what the keeper intends to do.

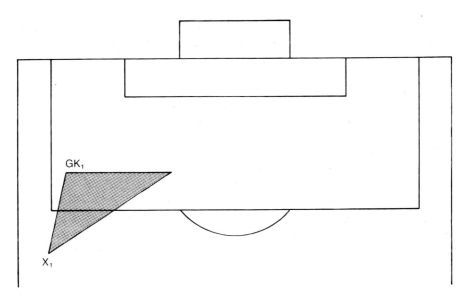

GK₁ is in a poor position because it does not give the defender any margin for error. If the ball is misdirected and played across the area, the results could be disastrous.

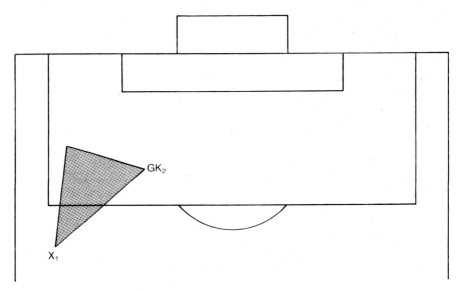

GK₂'s position is perfect because he is covering the possibility of a wayward pass across the area. At worst, a corner could be conceded.

Typical instructions for back passes are 'Keeper's on. Push it back!', 'Keeper's on. Early!', 'Keeper's on. Head it on!' and 'Keeper's on. Time!' The call for a back pass must be combined with support at the correct angle and distance so that the defender has little trouble.

Whenever defenders are in possession and are facing their own goal the keeper should help them to make the right decision. On the one hand they may be under severe pressure, necessitating an early back pass, and on the other they may have time to turn with the ball. The calls in these situations would vary from 'Keeper's on. Man on!' to 'Time. Turn!'

The goalkeeper should feel happy about manoeuvering his own defenders in order to protect his goal. If he feels that the attackers are being allowed too much space he must exhort his team-mates to mark them more closely. For example, he might call out 'Get tighter! or 'Close him down!'

One of the aims of defending is to force play in one direction so that it becomes predictable and easily dealt with. Information such as 'Tight!' Do not let him turn!' and 'Force him down the line!' will help to achieve that end. Furthermore, reminders to team-mates of basic defending principles, such as 'Close him down quickly!' or 'Stay on your feet!', will also assist the defensive unit in its job.

When the ball has been cleared the keeper should encourage his defence to push out to leave those forwards remaining in advanced positions off side. A loud cry of 'Push out!' or 'Squeeze up!' will suffice. He must always encourage the nearest player to pressurise the ball-carrier when the defensive unit is pushing up.

As soon as the ball crosses the half-way line the goalkeeper should be giving information and encouragement to other defenders. He should be mindful of the defence's objective to make play predictable by forcing the ball in one direction. As mentioned in Chapter 7, on the high cross the keeper must not allow defenders to drop too deep and thus deny him the space in which to attack the ball.

The timing and manner of the goalkeeper's communication is almost as important as the information he imparts. Early calls are absolutely essential because defenders already committed to a plan of action will not react well to late instructions. The information must be concise and easily understood. Precious seconds could be wasted by instructions that are long-winded. All information must be given in a loud, clear voice that instills confidence. An indecisive and nervous call can panic defenders and drain confidence. Even if the goalkeeper feels nervous inside he should try to exude calmness. He will achieve this if he provides early and relevant information in a confident and controlled manner.

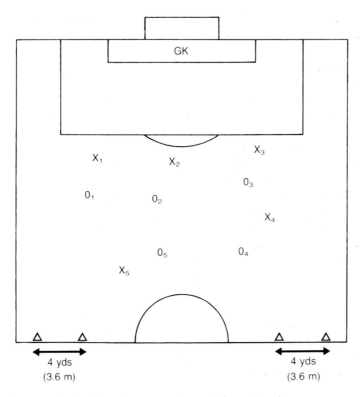

Practice for supporting the defence (see progression 1a on the next page).

Practice 1

The practice takes the form of a two against two plus two goalkeepers small-sided game in an area 30 yds × 20 yds (27 m × 18 m).

Key points
(a) Adopt a good starting position relative to the proximity of the ball.
(b) Keep in line with the ball.
(c) Be ready to deal with through balls.
(d) Support team-mates when in possession.
(e) Give clear information to team-mates when and where necessary.

Progression 1a

This practice takes place in one half of the field where five defenders (plus the goalkeeper) play against five attackers. The attackers have to score past the goalkeeper whereas the defenders have to pass the ball through one of two goals on the half-way line to register a goal. See the diagram on page 99.

Key points

(a)   Adopt a good starting position.
(b)   Keep in contact with the nearmost defender.
(c)   Support team-mates when they are in possession.
(d)   Impart quality information.
(e)   Inspire other defenders with confidence.

10   Organisation at set pieces

So many goals are scored from free kicks, corner kicks and throw-ins that it is vitally important for the goalkeeper and his team-mates to be adequately prepared. Rehearsal at training (or even before the game) of various strategies to combat certain set piece plays will reduce the number of goals conceded. Awareness of individual responsibilities at set pieces will mean that less is left to chance and the opposition will have to work hard for their goal.

Defending throw-ins

Short throws

There are basically two types of short throw. The first involves the thrower aiming the ball at a team-mate in his immediate vicinity. The idea is for the receiver either to turn with the ball or to play it back to the feet of the thrower who is then able to put in a cross. In order to counter this the keeper should ensure that all opponents in the vicinity are marked tightly and goal-side. In addition, a spare defender should be deployed in the space between the nearest attacker and the ball, thereby denying quality service from or back to the thrower. Defenders well away from the action do not have to mark so tightly because they have a responsibility for covering team-mates as well as looking after their opponent. The goalkeeper should be in the front half of his goal.

The other type of short throw involves the ball being played into a space created by two opponents making cross-over runs. By running towards each other and almost brushing shoulders as they pass, one or both of them lose their following markers and are then open to receive a pass. The solution for the marking players is either to spot the cross-over early and exchange players or to reduce the closeness of the marking at the point of the cross-over so that they are not blocked out.

The long throw

This can be quite a potent weapon because the trajectory of the ball is usually fairly low and does not allow the keeper much time to deal with it. Defenders can anticipate that opponents are preparing to use the long throw tactic because

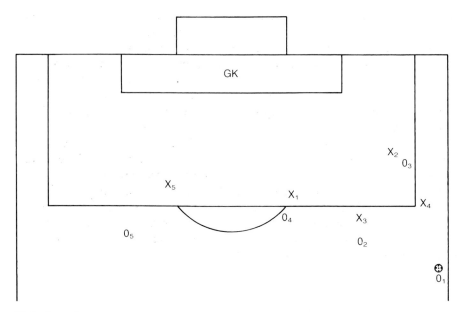

Defending a short throw.

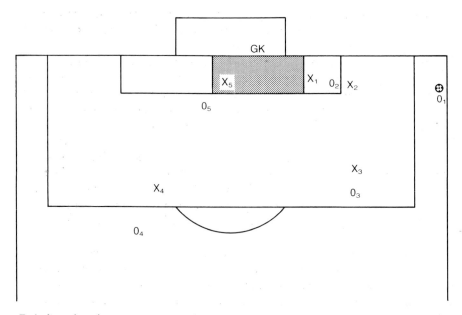

Defending a long throw.

they usually position a tall target player in the area between the near post and the junction of the six-yard box. Rather than scoring direct, this player will be aiming to get a slight touch on the ball for team-mates arriving in the space behind him. Once the ball has been flicked on, the defence has a problem.

Defensive arrangements should be made to prevent the target player gaining the vital first touch. The normal marking organisation should apply, with a tall defender marking behind the opponents' target player and another tallish defender marking in front.

If the attacker does make the flick on, the defence should then deal with the 'second ball'. The ball is likely to travel between 2–6 yds (2–5.5 m) behind the target player. Defenders should be ready to cover this area to prevent any secondary chances (*see* the shaded area in the lower diagram opposite).

The high, good length throw might allow the keeper the time to deal with the first ball. However, if the delivery is shorter and lower, the keeper might not have the time to claim the ball successfully. In that case, he should resist the temptation to attack and deal with the flick on instead.

Defending corners

There are two basic tactics employed in defending corners – man to man or zonal marking. I prefer zonal marking because it delegates specific areas of responsibility to defenders and the goalkeeper.

The corner played into the rear post is the most difficult to defend, so it is important that this area is well manned. One player (X1) covers the near post whilst two other defenders (X2 and X3) mark the space in front of the six-yard box. Other defenders are stationed at the middle and rear of the six-yard box. All the markers on the six-yard line are responsible for the space in front of them. The goalkeeper takes care of the area within his zone. It is important that the players marking zonally along the six-yard line are fairly tall and are good headers of the ball. Two players (X6 and X7) cover runs made from the back edge of the penalty area. Two smaller players (X8 and X9) deal with balls dropping in the area between the six-yard box and the edge of the penalty area. Positioning two players upfield will force the opposition to leave three players back to cover them.

If the opposition sends players deep into the six-yard box the keeper should not allow his own players to mark them. To do so would congest his area even further. The keeper must back his ability to beat opponents in the air, if not with a catch then at least with a punch. One advantage of zonal marking is that by delegating areas of reponsibility decision making becomes easier.

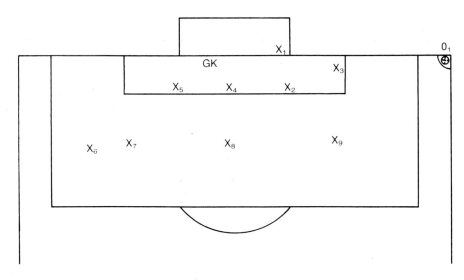

Defending a corner kick. Note the position of the goalkeeper in the rear of the goal.

If the opposition attempt a short corner, the whole defensive arrangement should shuffle over so that even though two defenders have been sent out to deal with the threat the near post area is not left exposed.

Defending free kicks around the penalty area

Free kicks conceded in and around the penalty area will necessitate forming a defensive wall, the purpose of which is to cover the part of the goal nearest to the ball. Guided by the defensive principle of forcing play in one direction, the wall is formed to discourage opponents from shooting directly at the nearest part of the goal. The goalkeeper, who should be positioned in the half of the goal not masked by the wall (so that he can see the ball), will be happy to deal with shots aimed in his direction because he is only covering a fraction of the goal.

The number of players in the wall is determined by the position of the free kick. Generally speaking, the nearer and more central the free kick the greater the number of players in the wall. As the distance of the free kick from the goal increases the number of players in the wall decreases. Excessive numbers should not be used in the wall because it reduces the amount of players free to carry out

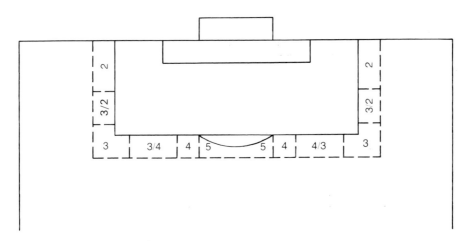

Deciding on the number of players in the wall.

marking jobs and gives the keeper less chance to see the ball.

All teams should have a defensive plan for dealing with free kicks. It is useful to give players positions in the wall. As defenders are usually more adept in marking, the wall is best left to designated midfield players.

As soon as the free kick is awarded the keeper should organise his defence acording to its rehearsed strategy. Skilful players will attempt to take the kick whilst the keeper is preoccupied with lining up the wall, so it is vitally important that the organisation is slick and takes as little time as possible.

The goalkeeper points out which side the wall should cover and decides upon the number of players in it. It is best to have the tallest player (X_1 in the top diagram overleaf) at the near post side in order to prevent the kicker chipping the ball over the end of the wall. The keeper lines up his end player with the near post and then instructs him to take half a step sideways in order to prevent a shot being swerved around the edge of the wall. Instructions should be clear and concise, for instance 'Move two yards to the right. Stop!' It is imperative that the goalkeeper does not stand behind the wall and thus obscure his view of the ball.

Occasionally the kicker will tap the ball inside to increase the shooting angle for another player. To counter this there should be a defensive charger (X_5) a yard or so off the end of the wall who will quickly pressurise the ball if it is played sideways. Other defenders should be used to mark opponents elsewhere in the area.

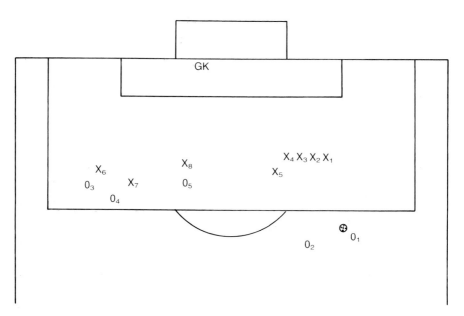

Organisation at a central free kick.

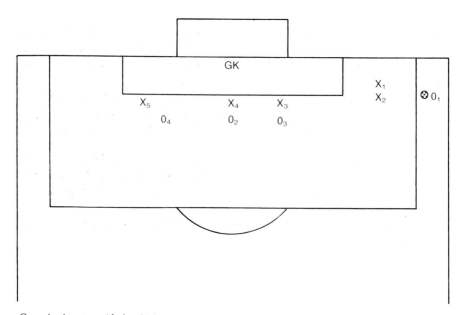

Organisation at a wide free kick.

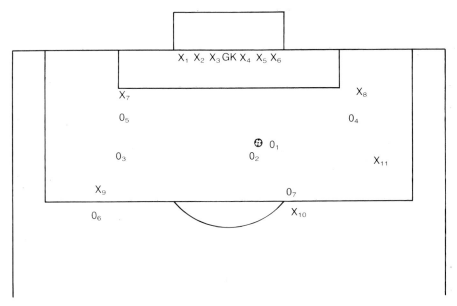

Organisation for a free kick conceded inside the area.

With this arrangement the keeper can prepare himself to receive a direct shot in his half of the goal. If the ball is chipped over or swerved around the wall it will not be hit with pace and therefore will give the keeper time to move across and save.

For free kicks in wider positions the wall will not only prevent a direct shot but will also deny the kicker the opportunity to drive in a low cross. The player will be forced to lift the ball and this will give the defence more time to clear the danger.

For those indirect free kicks conceded inside the area it may be necessary to pull all players back to defend. If the kick is awarded within 12 yds (11 m) of the goal, it is advisable to have a six or seven player wall with the keeper in the middle. As soon as the kick is taken the wall should converge on the ball with the intention of blocking the shot. Spare defenders should be used to mark opponents in the penalty area.

Practices for defending throws, corners and free kicks

These practices can take place in an eleven-a-side game. The coach can either wait until throw-ins, corners and free kicks occur naturally or award them arbitrarily throughout the game. Points to look for may include the following.

(a) Alertness when the ball is out of play. 'When the ball is dead, be alive.'
(b) Rapid and slick organisation.
(c) Awareness of individual and collective responsibilities.

When the worth of set piece organisation has been proved in training and reinforced by the coach, players will react automatically in real match situations.

11   Saving penalties

Every goalkeeper dreams of saving a penalty in a cup final and being mobbed by joyous team-mates. A saved penalty can turn a game and can break the spirit of the opposition, so it is worth examining some of the strategies used by keepers when faced with a penalty kick. If the keeper can hit upon a technique that brings him regular success, then he should stick with it.

Except for very young players it is extremely difficult for a keeper to save a penalty without first having decided to commit himself to one side or the other. Although Law XIV (taken from the *Referees' Chart and Player's Guide to the Laws of Association Football 1988–9,* Pan, 1988) states that 'The goalkeeper must stand (without moving his feet) on the goal-line between the goal-posts until the ball is kicked', most penalties are saved as a result of the keeper moving early. The majority of referees will give the benefit of the doubt to the keeper as long as this early movement is not too great.

Penalty saving techniques

Assessing the type of player taking the kick

Generally speaking, defenders take fewer risks than midfield or forward players and tend to play safe by pushing the ball to the same side as the kicking foot.

Tricky, skilful players may try to fool the goalkeeper by clipping the ball to the opposite side of the kicking foot. It is worth noting that left-footed players tend to favour that method.

Watching the eyes of the kicker

As soon as the kick is awarded the keeper watches the eyes of the kicker looking for some indication as to which side he will place his kick.

Trying to dummy the kicker

As the player runs up to take the kick the keeper makes an exaggerated body movement (without moving the feet) to one side. The object is to make the

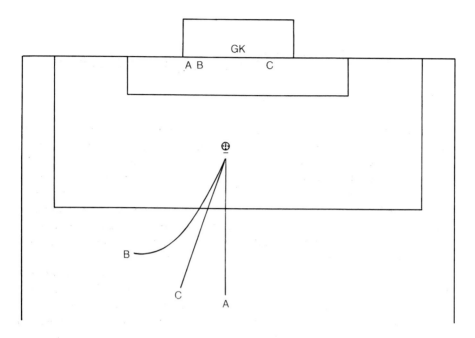

Penalty technique.

kicker think that the keeper is going to dive that way. As a result, he places the ball on the other side – right into the arms of the goalkeeper.

Observing the approach of the kicker

The run-up of the kicker can give some idea of his body position as he strikes the ball and therefore an indication of where the ball is intended to go. If the player addresses the ball from a head-on and very straight approach, then it is likely that the natural swing will make him aim to the opposite side to the kicking foot (A in the diagram above). If the approach is curved (B), it is probable that the result will be the same. However, if the approach is straight but slightly off-centre (C), it is likely that the final body position will be open and the shot placed to the same side as the kicking foot.

12　Conditioning exercises

Conditioning (alternatively known as fitness training), like coaching, is a means to an end. Unless it results in improving match performance it is pointless. Players who wish to fulfil their potential must ensure that they are fully equipped to meet the demands of the modern game. To put it another way, players should not be able to blame poor preparation for a sub-standard performance. The importance of a thorough coaching programme and pre-match warm-up has already been discussed, but this will be negated if players are not physically capable of sustaining a desirable level of performance. Consequently, the coach should be aware of the fitness needs of all of his players.

Reaching peak fitness and then maintaining it is not easy and is not without its share of discomfort. There is a saying 'No pain, no gain' which contains a large element of truth. Players must work hard in training throughout the season because fitness is not like a bank account that accrues interest when left alone. It has to be constantly topped up or the level will diminish. The key to maintaining fitness is motivation. If training is enjoyable, purposeful and competitive, players will be motivated to push themselves so that fitness benefits result.

As fitness is so important, the coach must not approach the question haphazardly. The whole programme should be carefully planned and should reflect the following process.

(a)　Identification of training needs – these differ according to the type and playing position of individuals.
(b)　Implementation of a varied training programme based on quality rather than quantity of work.
(c)　Regular objective monitoring of fitness during training sessions. This can be done reliably via time trials, circuit training, etc.
(d)　Regular subjective evaluation of fitness levels during matches.

Implications for the goalkeeper

Goalkeepers require an all-round fitness. They need to have nimble feet and good spring, but also the upper body strength to cope with the hardest of shots and the strongest of physical challenges. In addition, they ought to possess the suppleness and speed of reaction to deal with the unexpected. All of these qualities need to be founded upon a good level of basic cardio-vascular fitness.

In order to make the work realistic and enjoyable a ball should be used as much as possible. However, it is imperative that the coach knows the difference between coaching and training. Many people wrongly assume that goalkeeping coaching is pressure training (rapid repetitions of a particular exercise). Skill levels will break down once fatigue sets in, so when coaching a particular technique the keeper needs time to digest the key factors if he is to carry out the practice successfully. With pressure training there is little time for such reflection and within a few minutes the player is too exhausted to perform the technique in the desired manner. Pressure training has its uses in improving stamina and strength, but not in the perfection of technique.

I have identified four fitness areas for goalkeepers and provided a selection of exercises for each. It is recommended that fitness work occurs after concentrating on technical aspects.

Stamina

The goalkeeper should not be excused from the running drills involving outfield players for he, too, requires good sprinting speed and a reasonable level of endurance.

Exercise 1

The keeper lies flat on his stomach and the coach throws the ball into the air. The keeper has to leap to his feet and catch the ball at the highest point possible. The exercise should be repeated rapidly ten times.

Exercise 2

The keeper has to glide in between markers arranged in a zig-zag manner. The coach shoots as the keeper reaches the final marker. After saving, he jogs back to the beginning. The exercise is repeated ten times.

Exercise 3

The coach arranges ten balls around the edge of the six-yard box. Starting at one end, he shoots in rapid succession. The keeper has to save as many shots as possible. After a brief rest the exercise is repeated, with the keeper trying to improve on his previous score.

Exercise 4

This exercise involves three goals – two five-yard goals located 15 yds (13.75 m) from the by-line on each side of the goal and a full size goal. The keeper, starting from his near post, approaches goal A and player S1 forces him to make a sharp save. The keeper has to recover immediately and look to save from S2 shooting at goal B. He then touches the far post and approaches goal C to make another sharp save from S3. The keeper has one final shot to save from S2 aiming for goal B. The exercise is repeated five times (with rests in between) and is conducted at high speed.

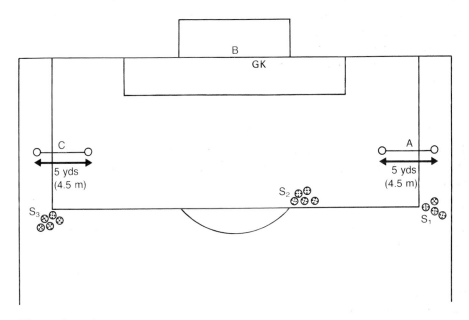

Three-goal practice.

Exercise 5

Two servers stand level with a post 6–7 yds (5.5–6.5 m) from the goal, armed with four footballs each. One server feeds the ball low towards the post so that the keeper is forced to make a diving save. As he gets up the second server feeds high towards the other post. The keeper has to move quickly to save. This process is repeated until all the footballs have been used. After a short rest the exercise is repeated.

Sharpness

Exercise 1
The keeper stands with his legs open facing a server standing two to three yards away who passes the ball through his legs. The keeper has to spin and dive on the ball. The exercise is repeated ten times.

Exercise 2
The keeper stands with his legs open, facing away from a server standing at a distance of two to three yards. The server passes the ball through his legs. The keeper has to dive on the ball as it appears. The exercise is repeated ten times.

Exercise 3
The goalkeeper faces his goal. On the command from the server (standing 6–12 yds (5.5–11 m) away) he turns and is met by a shot. This exercise is repeated in two sets of ten.

Exercise 4
The goalkeeper faces out to S1 who feeds by hand to S2. S2 then volleys the ball towards the near-side part of the goal. The goalkeeper has to react and make the save. This exercise is repeated in two sets of ten.

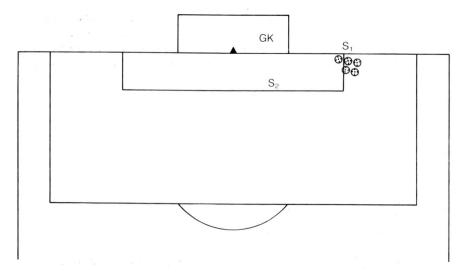

Reaction save practice.

Suppleness

Exercise 1
With the ball in his hands the goalkeeper does a forward roll and returns to his feet in one movement. This exercise is repeated six times.

Exercise 2
Sitting on the ground, the goalkeeper has to catch balls delivered to alternate sides by a server standing two to three yards away.

Exercise 3
The goalkeeper lies flat on his stomach and the server feeds the ball from a distance of one to two yards so that the keeper is forced to arch his back to make the catch. The exercise is repeated ten times.

Exercise 4
The goalkeeper sits on the floor and the server feeds the ball to alternate sides. After each save the goalkeeper must thrust himself forwards without using his hands. Rhythmic feeding by the server will help the keeper move his trunk from the goal-line to the edge of the penalty area. The exercise is repeated after a rest.

Exercise 5
The goalkeeper lies on his back with a server three yards either side of him. One server rolls the ball towards the keeper and he has to take evasive action so that it carries on unimpeded to the other server. The keeper can let the ball pass through by sitting up, arching his back or lifting his legs. The exercise is repeated twenty times.

Strength

Exercise 1
A choice of one of the following:

(a) ordinary press-ups (3 × 25)
(b) press-ups on the knuckles (3 × 25)
(c) press-ups on the fingers (3 × 15)
(d) press-ups on the football (3 × 10)
(e) 1 press-up; clap hands: 2 press-ups; clap hands: 3 press-ups; clap hands and so on until you reach 10 press-ups.

Exercise 2
Regular squeezing of a squash or tennis ball. This can be done every day whilst watching television, sitting on the bus, and so on.

Exercise 3
Using the right leg, the keeper hops from his goal to the half-way line in as few hops as possible. The same procedure is repeated for left leg and bunny hops. The whole exercise is repeated, with the keeper trying to beat his previous score.

Exercise 4
With one knee on the floor, the keeper tries to stand up without touching the toes of the trailing leg on the ground. This exercise is repeated five times for each leg.

Exercise 5
Lying on his back, the keeper rolls back and gets to his feet without using his hands, knees or elbows for assistance. The exercise is repeated ten times.

Exercise 6
Sitting with the feet raised 12 in (30 cm) from the ground, the keeper has to catch balls fed to alternate sides by a server standing two to three yards away. The exercise is repeated thirty times.

13 The eight 'Cs' to goalkeeping success

The aim of goalkeeping is to keep the ball out of the net, and if the keeper manages to do this safely and consistently using unorthodox techniques his 'style' must not be coached out of him. The purpose of this book is to help the goalkeeper carry out his job effectively, not to attain marks for artistic merit. So, if a keeper's method is successful game after game the coach should not attempt to change it. My advice to youngsters is to observe and appreciate the top goalkeepers but be wary of imitating them. Young players should develop their own style based on an awareness of their own strengths and limitations.

I become irritated when people discount promising young goalkeepers because they are 'too small'. All keepers have their strengths and weaknesses and a short player's strong points might be a taller person's failing. If the goalkeeper is winning matches rather than making glaring errors, his height will not be an important factor.

In an attempt to determine what makes a good goalkeeper I have identified eight interdependent key areas – the eight 'Cs'.

Confidence

Confidence is the foundation on which all other aspects of goalkeeping are built. Without it the keeper will not approach the job in a positive manner, performances will become erratic and his team will be burdened with an unreliable keeper. In the goalkeeping context confidence is an unfailing belief in one's ability, despite the occasional setback. Inevitably mistakes will be made, but the good player puts them at the back of his mind and continues unaffected for the rest of the game. The uncertain keeper fails to come to terms with error and, doubting his ability, fails to perform to his full potential. What he must remember is that one mistake does not mean that he has suddenly become a poor player. Indeed, a more accurate indicator of his worth can be observed in his response after the error has been made. In short, the only thing that the goalkeeper has to fear is fear itself.

A goalkeeper should never show that he is frightened because that hands the initiative to the opposition. Even if he feels nervous he should give the impression of being in total control both of himself and of his fellow defenders. Such a display will inspire self-confidence and the confidence of those around him.

During those off-form periods when the goalkeeper feels confidence draining away he should recall games in which he has performed well and relive them repeatedly in his mind. By visualising these memories the keeper will build up a positive picture of himself and his abilities. This rekindled self-esteem will help to dissipate the fear and negative attitude caused by a loss of form. It is at these times that the coach can play a vital role in maintaining the keeper's self-esteem. Constant encouragement allied to appropriate coaching practice will accelerate the return to peak performance.

Competence

All players should work conscientiously at improving their skill level. This will entail polishing their strong points until they catch the eye and working hard to rectify weaknesses.

The goalkeeper's training schedule should revolve around reducing the number of mistakes made during matches. As mistakes are caused by technical errors or wrong decisions it should be fairly easy to identify where problems are occurring. Training sessions should be spent concentrating on those areas causing the keeper concern so that he has the opportunity to correct any faults appearing in his game. However, he should still devote some time to working on the 'bread and butter' areas of head, hands and feet because mastery of the basics will make the difficult saves look easy.

Although there is no substitute for match experience in assisting the learning process, the training sessions should stretch the keeper so that a high level of skill and commitment is demanded. Good habits in training will spread to match performance and, as competence grows, the keeper will radiate confidence.

Concentration

It only takes a split second to let in a goal, so if the keeper 'switches off' during a game the result could be disastrous. Unlike outfield players, the keeper cannot go off in pursuit of the ball searching for action. The extent to which he is occupied depends on how successful the opposition is in getting the ball close to his goal. Generally speaking, it is easier to perform effectively when constantly involved in the action rather than when called upon to make a save only once in a while. When inactive for long spells it is essential that the goalkeeper maintains a high level of concentration and tries to involve himself in the game as much as possible. Even when play is in the opponents' half he can be constantly adjusting his position ready for a quick breakaway, and of course he can keep in touch with play by being a source of information for the defenders in front of him.

The key to good concentration is taking nothing for granted and being primed for action at all times. This means treating every shot (even back passes) with respect and being prepared for defensive lapses or individual brilliance from opponents.

Competitiveness

All goalkeepers should be determined not to be beaten and if they are it should be a momentary personal tragedy. Unless the keeper is prepared to go to inordinate lengths (including risking personal safety) in order to prevent a goal he will never be successful. A strong competitive streak will result in a positive approach to the game and will boost confidence. As stated earlier, I believe the way in which a keeper performs is more important than his physical characteristics. If the keeper believes he is a giant who has to dominate his area, he will play like one, irrespective of size. Like confidence, this will to win is infectious and a keeper can inspire his defenders with the same determination to keep his goal intact.

It is important that players are also competitive in training because it is not a quality that can be turned on like a tap for matches. The determination not to concede a goal must be a permanent feature of the keeper's make-up. A contempt for being beaten will result in a conscientious approach to training and will ensure that areas of weakness are attended to.

Consistency

One of the qualities that top goalkeepers possess is the ability to perform to a high standard game in, game out. Keepers who have proved their reliability over a number of matches will be greatly valued by their team. Being consistent entails carrying out the job efficiently with very few costly mistakes.

The key to consistency is the religious application of the basics, coupled with good decision making in every game whatever the prevailing conditions or quality of opposition. This requires considerable powers of concentration because there will be days when the keeper feels below par and his mind starts wandering. He must prevent this by harnessing his competitive instincts in such a way that all he thinks about during the game is keeping the ball out of the net. Good preparation can enhance concentration so that the mind and body are tuned in ready to make a save as soon as the game starts.

The enemy of consistency is complacency. The moment that the keeper starts taking the game for granted he will be embarrassed. He must treat every game, every shot and every cross in the same respectful way. Complacency breeds sloppiness which, in turn, leads to mistakes. From the time that he arrives at the ground until the end of the match the keeper should devote his mind and energies to keeping the ball out of the net.

Courage

There are bound to be occasions during matches when the keeper, in an attempt to prevent a goal, risks injury. These situations demand raw courage inspired by the desire not to be beaten. However, if the keeper applies the correct technique and commits himself fully to the physical confrontation, serious injury should seldom result. In any case, most keepers feel more pain when the ball hits the back of the net than when personally taking a physical knock. Often the keeper's courage can turn the game, as we can see from the following equation:

courage + competence + competitiveness = match-winning save.

Courage of a different sort is the mental strength to make crucial decisions. For instance, when conditions are muddy and the opposition aggressive it is easier to stay on the line than to come for a high cross. However, the keeper has to back his ability and make the correct decision. This mental courage will be tested to the full during those times when confidence is low and negative tendencies predominate over the positive. Form will only be rediscovered by conquering fear and making the correct decisions.

Communication

As the last line of defence the goalkeeper is perfectly placed to view the whole game as it unfolds in front of him. Consequently, he should be a constant source of information and encouragement for his team. Through good use of his voice he can make his team-mates aware of unforeseen dangers and ensure that the defence is well organised. For this reason it is important that the goalkeeper knows what, how and when to communicate.

A clear early call can result in a blind-side run being picked up or it can help a defender decide upon a course of action when under pressure. Given in the correct manner and at the appropriate time, intelligent information can nip potentially dangerous situations in the bud. This ability to communicate effectively comes with the experience which in turn is born out of an open-minded and conscientious approach to the game.

Coaching

Coaching is about accelerating the learning process. If all the aforementioned personal attributes are equal, then it will be the quality of coaching that will determine whether a player stands out from his peers. The good coach will bring out the best in the goalkeeper, nurturing what natural talent he possesses through well structured practices. Without such guidance an individual's development is left to chance and the cultivation of bad habits will remain unchecked.

14 Final advice

All successful goalkeepers have a single-minded determination to keep the ball out of the net. It is this commitment which drives them to practise hard to perfect their craft. Honest self-appraisal is important if the goalkeeper is to recognise those areas of his game that require special attention. Moreover, an accurate estimate of his strengths and limitations will result in better decision-making.

The goalkeeper owes it to himself and to his team to be at his peak mentally as well as physically for match play. This will not only involve working hard in training, but also approaching the game in the correct manner.

In both training and match play the keeper should concentrate on reducing the number of technical errors he makes. However, he should remember that there are occasions when application of the perfect technique is impossible and an untidy save is the only option left. The keeper must never lose sight of the fact that his job is to keep the ball out of the net, and if he mishandles a shot he must make a secondary save. Many goalkeepers, angry at not making a clean catch, lose concentration after dropping the ball and fail to regain possession immediately. This can, of course, prove disastrous.

Above all, the keeper should aim to be consistent, which entails resisting the tendency to become complacent during good spells as well as working extra hard when form is poor. It is a useful analogy to compare good performances with deposits in a bank. When the goalkeeper enjoys an error-free game he makes a deposit, while poor performances give no return. Aiming to reach a pre-determined number of deposits can motivate the keeper to perform well game after game.

A goalkeeping check-list

1. Constantly practise handling and footwork skills.
2. Keep physically fit.
3. Prepare correctly for every game.
4. Be positive.
5. Treat every shot with respect.
6. Never switch off during games.

7. Develop good communication with fellow defenders.
8. Be organised at set pieces.
9. Take good care of equipment.
10. Never lose faith in your ability.

Points to remember for the coach

Starting from the recognition that the goalkeeper occupies the single most important position in the team, the coach should ensure that the keeper is given sufficient time in which to practise his craft. Merely completing a training session with a shooting drill will not satisfy a keeper's needs. He should have a personalised coaching programme aimed at polishing his strengths and minimising his weaknesses.

Basics

All training sessions should incorporate work on the basis – head, hands, feet – so that good habits are firmly established. In addition, the coach should be able to identify areas of concern from match play, and should then arrange a session which concentrates on those aspects. The coaching session should begin at a level where the keeper experiences some success before progressing to increasingly realistic and difficult practice situations. This progression from the easy to the difficult will help improve the keeper's confidence as well as his competence.

Confidence building

The coach should aim to make each training session as positive as possible so that the keeper leaves the pitch confident in his ability and fully prepared for the next match. One way of doing this is to end the session with a save which leaves the goalkeeper with a favourable self-image.

Good ball feeding

The feeding of the ball during training sessions is very important, too, as it is soul-destroying to be constantly retrieving the ball from the back of the net during practices. The coach should tailor his serving so that it brings out the best in his goalkeeper, not in himself. High levels of performance will not be attained if the keeper approaches the game in a negative frame of mind.

Practice for the substitute keeper

In the small-sided game which usually rounds off a training session the coach should give the team's emergency keeper experience of playing in goal. All teams should have an outfield player who can replace the goalkeeper if he has to leave the field, and if this player has received some coaching in goalkeeping skills he will be better equipped to meet the emergency.

Outfield practice

At the same time, it is also a useful exercise to allow the goalkeeper to play in the outfield during the small-sided game. Most teams expect their goalkeeper to act as a sweeper and to venture outside his area to deal with potentially dangerous situations. As this often necessitates good levels of control, experience of outfield play in training will give the keeper confidence to leave his area if the situation demands.

Summary

Ideally, coaching sessions should include the following elements.

1. Work on basic techniques.
2. Practice on areas of concern.
3. Game situations incorporating (a) decision-making
(b) co-operation with other defenders.
4. Rehearsal of organisation at set pieces.

Boosting morale

Finally, it is important that players enjoy their football. The coach can encourage this enjoyment by making training sessions stimulating, valuing the players' abilities and praising good play. Praise is a better motivator than criticism and a few well chosen words can do wonders for a player's morale.

As the position in which they play is such a pressurised one, goalkeepers find it difficult to enjoy the game while it is in progress. Therefore, their enjoyment tends to be retrospective. It is later on, when he has time to unwind and analyse his performancce, that the keeper can look back on the game and his performance either with pride or with embarrassment and shame. Generally speaking, saves which required some decision-making provide more pleasure for the keeper than purely instinctive ones. There is no better feeling than relaxing after a match reflecting upon a job well done.

Index